TECH BILLIONAIRE$

TECH BILLIONAIRE$

Reshaping Philanthropy in a Quest for a Better World

Lewis D. Solomon

Transaction Publishers
New Brunswick (U.S.A.) and London (U.K.)

Copyright © 2009 by Transaction Publishers, New Brunswick, New Jersey.

All rights reserved under International and Pan-American Copyright Conventions. No part of this book may be reproduced or transmitted in any form or by any means, electronic or mechanical, including photocopy, recording, or any information storage and retrieval system, without prior permission in writing from the publisher. All inquiries should be addressed to Transaction Publishers, Rutgers—The State University of New Jersey, 35 Berrue Circle, Piscataway, New Jersey 08854-8042. www.transactionpub.com

This book is printed on acid-free paper that meets the American National Standard for Permanence of Paper for Printed Library Materials.

Library of Congress Catalog Number: 2008031098
ISBN: 978-1-4128-0847-7
Printed in the United States of America

        Library of Congress Cataloging-in-Publication Data

Solomon, Lewis D.
  Tech billionaires : reshaping philanthropy in a quest for a better world / Lewis D. Solomon.
      p. cm.
  Includes bibliographical references and index.
  ISBN 978-1-4128-0847-7 (acid-free paper)
    1. Philanthropists--United States--Case studies. 2. Charities--United States--Case studies. 3. Endowments--United States--Case studies. 4. Rich people--Charitable contributions--United States--Case studies. I. Title.

HV27.S65 2008
361.7'4092273--dc22

                                                      2008031098

For Walter F. LaFeber,
who guided me in the craft of writing

Table of Contents

Foreword		ix
1.	Introduction	1
2.	Private Foundations in the United States: The Impact of Andrew Carnegie and John D. Rockefeller Sr.	9
3.	Bill and Melinda Gates Foundation: Big Goals but Following the Traditional Foundation Model	15
4.	Pierre Omidyar and Omidyar Network: Pioneering Hybrid Philanthropy	43
5.	Jeffrey Skoll and His Philanthropic Endeavors: Funding Social Entrepreneurs and Motion Pictures	67
6.	Stephen Case: The Rise and Fall of a Business Empire, Then Entrepreneurship and Innovative Philanthropy	85
7.	Sergey Brin, Larry Page, and *Google.org:* The Corporation as Philanthropist	107
8.	Conclusion	125
Index		137

Foreword

Tech Billionaires is an important book for the public at large and for the philanthropic community.

As Americans we are fascinated by extreme wealth. We try to imagine what life would be like if we took home the tens of millions each year that many corporate executives and baseball players make, let alone the hundreds of millions that are not uncommon for hedge fund managers and TV stars. How would we spend that much money beyond paying off our debt?

The annual lists of the 50 or 100 wealthiest people and their charity, more often than philanthropy, shows a pattern of giving that seems more directed to their naming rights than to social change. Here is [Sanford] Weill Cornell Medical College. The New York Public Library building has stood protected by its lions on Fifth Avenue in New York since 1911 without the names of philanthropists John Jacob Astor, James Lenox, and Samuel Tilden who made it happen. But in 2008 Blackstone Hedge Fund co-founder Stephen A. Schwarzman, whose wealth was estimated at $7.6 billion in 2007, got his name in five places for only $200,000 per plaque. Their gifts result in endowed and named chairs and special institutes at the already heavily endowed universities in the U.S. and around the world, and in named art collections in many museums. The donors receive recognition forever (unless, of course, they prove to have obtained their wealth through misbegotten gains, such as Dennis Kozlowski of Tyco notoriety, at which point the concrete comes out to fill in the letters, or the screw driver to remove the plaque). Society benefits, they the donors benefit, but social change is not their goal.

As an antidote to excess without apparent purpose, these chapters illuminate the drive of a group of "tech billionaires" to make the world a better place. Their wealth comes from activities that tread relatively lightly on the environment. Their motivation does not seem to arise from a need to account for previous sins, as was the case with some of the earlier large philanthropic donors, and many today.

Philanthropy also has a fascination with size: "My endowment is bigger than yours and my giving is greater." The weekly list serve of the Foundation Center rarely includes a grant of less than $100,000, and the *Chronicle of Philanthropy's* bi-weekly lists are weighted to larger grants. Obviously there are space limitations but grant size almost always seems to win out over substance.

In addition to the size of these new philanthropies, the speed with which they appeared and established their mark in fields where other donors were long established, and beyond, is remarkable. Money does talk. These newcomers were certainly not shy.

A full assessment of the style, substance, and effectiveness of these new funds, most of them only a decade or so old, will come in time. Not bound by philanthropic traditions they have moved quickly to define their space. Lewis Solomon has captured their story at a moment in time, and laid the groundwork for a fuller assessment in the years to come.

Reading the manuscript provoked me to think about some of the issues, old and new, that an assessment of the philanthropies of the billionaires, and philanthropy as a whole, will need to address.

What is the purpose of philanthropy?

I believe that the primary purpose of philanthropy is to hold institutions in society accountable to the needs of the commonweal. The goal is to assist in a variety of ways to ensure a functioning democracy that is environmentally sound, and socially and economically just.[1] Charity is not philanthropy.

Foundations have generously responded to natural disasters, as evidenced by the funds made available to Hurricane Katrina victims. But how much was done to awaken a still indolent government that has failed its people?

What is the nature of change?

Philanthropy should be able to define the nature of the changes to be achieved along a continuum:

- Within the social and economic system lies amelioration, mitigation, adaptation, and reformation;
- Outside the system lies transformation and revolution.

Embedded in both of the two questions is the issue of "government by philanthropy." This is where the larger foundations, including the "tech billionaires," provide funds for services that could/should be the responsibility of governments or intergovernmental organizations. Pressing governments to act in a nonpartisan way about an issue is legal. But now the tech philanthropies can set an agenda of their own that could skew the agendas of governments and intergovernmental institutions that have a more open process. Gates has been criticized by the World Health Organization for "stifling a diversity of views among scientists and wiping out the world health agency's policy-making function [on malaria]."[2] Their grants for health in Africa are admirable given the weakness of governments in the region, but are they sustainable? Can they build physical and financial infrastructures that will carry on when the grants leave? If history is a reliable guide, the outlook is not promising.

What use is made of the foundations' assets and the billionaires' assets to add value to their grant dollars?

At most foundations there is an artificial wall between investment and grantmaking.[3] Jeff Skoll, Pierre Omydar, and *Google.org* appear to have seen the value added, whereas for Bill Gates there have been problems.[4] That may result from the absence of a bright line between Microsoft and the Gates Foundation. But these billions need to be used twice: to provide the money for grants *and* to add value to these grants through the investment process and shareowner activity.

Can a foundation be too big?

The Gates Foundation must spend enormous amounts for grants each day. Inevitably this leads to large grants that can inhibit creativity and foster conservatism, possibly diverting public resources to tasks that were not on their agendas. Certain areas so important for sustaining democracy, such as community organizing, cannot be on the agenda. While these community organizations have real needs, but few philanthropic donors, they cannot absorb the large sums that many of the big foundations need to process each year. There should be a window for them, too, to obtain a portion of this largesse.

What is the problem?

James Gustav Speth, now dean of Yale's School of Forestry, has had a long and varied career at the intersection of the environment and policy. In his new book, *Bridge at the Edge of the World: Capitalism, the Environment, and the Crossing from Crisis to Sustainability*, he concludes

After much searching and considerable reluctance, . . . that most environmental deterioration is a result of systemic failures of the capitalism we have today and that long-term solutions must seek transformative change in the key features of contemporary capitalism.[5]

He joins a long line of activists and scholars who have gone well beyond transformation of the capitalist system to call for a new "ism" that values equity and justice, as well as the environment.

Accepting his Nobel Prize in 1974 the conservative economist Frederick Hayek observed the irony of his receiving the prize for offering solutions to problems that economists had created.

If the problem is free market capitalism what role can these tech billionaires play in finding solutions? How much can microfinance achieve over the long term to bring people out of poverty? Bill Gates' "creative capitalism" does not change the underlying economic and social structure of a capitalist system and its impacts on the poor. An alliance with businesses works in some circumstances, such as achieving a lower price for AIDS drugs. But for communities, particularly people of color and poor communities in the U.S. and overseas, that are the object of corporate indifference and excesses, collaboration cannot begin until their needs are heard and addressed.

Feast on this book and make your own lists.

—Stephen Viederman, President (1986-2000) Jessie Smith Noyes Foundation; Current Member of Finance Committees–Christopher Reynolds Foundation and Needmor Fund

Notes

1. Stephen Viederman, Philanthropy and Democracy, *EGA News*, Fall 2006, 27-28; and Stephen Viederman, *Philanthropy New Zealand News*, Vol. 2, No. 40, Summer 2005, pages 14-16.
2. Donald G. McNeil Jr., Gates Foundation's Influence Criticized. *New York Times*, February 16, 2008.
3. Stephen Viederman, How Grantmakers Can Curb Global Warming, *The Chronicle of Philanthropy*, February 7, 2008; and Stephen Viederman, Get Off Your Assets for Climate, *Green Giving: The Newsletter of the Climate Change Philanthropy Action Network*, May 2008.
4. See a series of articles by Charles Pillar at the *Los Angeles Times* beginning in January 2007.
5. Yale University Press, 2008. Speth has been chair of the U.S. Council of Environmental Advisers, founder and president of the World Resources Institute, and administrator of the UNDP.

1

Introduction

Over the last decade a new wave of thinking has emerged from tech billionaires that could shape the way private capital gets invested to tackle social problems. These entrepreneurs broke the business mold in the 1980s and 1990s and are now trying to break the traditional pattern of philanthropy pioneered by Andrew Carnegie and John D. Rockefeller Sr., some one hundred years ago. Combining billions of dollars of their personal capital with new ideas, cutting-edge businesslike techniques, media and marketing savvy, the tech benefactors profiled in this book are attacking some of the globe's most intractable societal problems. In trying to make a difference in the world, these new philanthropists dubbed philanthrocapitalists, seek to break down the traditional barriers dividing business, charity, and government.

Beyond their blockbuster donations, they have something different in mind than traditional giving. Through their innovative approaches, they are changing the structure of philanthropy, by combining market-based techniques, even profit-making ones, with their charitable notions.

As a result of the rapid wealth creation in recent years, the world now boasts 1,125 billionaires, some sixty percent of whom are self-made, according to *Forbes'* 2008 list.[1] Their massive wealth has created new philanthropic challenges. Imaginative giving by the new billionaires is beginning to transform philanthropy in terms of: timing; involvement; strategy; and tactics.

Timing of Gifts. The new billionaires, particularly those who made their fortunes in technology, are giving while living. They are handing over the bulk of their fortunes during their lifetime, not making promises to be fulfilled by bequests on their death. They are sharing their wealth at midlife, rather than in their wills, thereby heralding a new style of giving, so that they can take part in achieving their goals and helping solve the worst problems plaguing society.

When billionaire Jeffrey S. Skoll, the former president of eBay, was fifteen, his father came home one day and announced to the family that he was seriously ill with cancer. What bothered his father the most was not the thought of dying, but that he had not done the things he wanted to do with his life. "That had a huge impact on me," Skoll recalled. Although his father survived the health crisis, Skoll indicated, "I realize time is fleeting. I didn't want to wait till it was too late to do something with my life."[2]

The tech billionaires profiled in this book are giving away vast portions of their wealth while they are still able to oversee where the money goes and how it is used. They seek to make certain their gifts effectively fund causes they have chosen, rather than trusting future foundation heads (or trustees), who may stray from their designated missions.

Involvement. The tech billionaires are fully engaged philanthropists. They want to be directly involved in how their money is spent. They run their philanthropic endeavors in the same hands-on way they ran their businesses. Seeing themselves as investors, they want to apply the best elements of the for-profit world to their giving so as to maximize its social return, at least as each one sees it.

The new philanthropists seek to employ the same smarts and diligence that made them rich. They are finding new ways to increase the efficiency of their giving and measure returns. They bring with them businesslike rigor, MBAs-metrics, an emphasis on scalability, tough evaluation techniques, and willingness to take risks but stop funding projects that are not performing as they had hoped. Many work as hard at giving their money away as they did at making it.

In their giving, the tech billionaires often strive to be partners, not mere patrons. Finding one or more issues of great personal significance, the new philanthropists may place large "bets" on a limited number of projects they regard as effective and introduce performance measurement techniques to assess their success, including agreed-on timelines, specific benchmarks, and mandatory impact reports. Rather than handing over their money to others to spend, they are involved in key funding decisions, bringing a pragmatic business approach to their giving. With their hands-on approach, they work with grantees to help them achieve their aims by providing continuing advice on a variety of management-oriented topics, including strategy, organizational development, and performance. In short, the new philanthropists want to apply the best elements of the for-profit world to their giving. They also see their task as forging alliances and building networks with government and business as well as other donor-foundations and nonprofit recipients.

Following the path of Carnegie and Rockefeller, for some philanthropy becomes a second career. They bring to it the same discipline and talent they used to accumulate their fortunes. Their demands for measurable results, efficiency, and greater openness and disclosure will reverberate throughout the nonprofit world.

Strategy. In bringing discipline and organization to the field, the tech billionaires try to match their philanthropic capital with a desire to meet urgent social needs. They want to mobilize and deploy private resources to improve our world. They want to attack problems of human suffering now, rather than later.

They seek to use their wealth to battle vexing societal ills from disease to poverty to global warming. They generally want to avoid hoarding their assets to create financial dynasties. Tales of offspring who became dilettante loafers terrify many.

Because some of the world's most pressing problems are far beyond America's borders, they funnel money to projects overseas. They work globally, strive to build programs, not edifices, and often focus on those absolutely the worst off.

Using their capital strategically, they want to maximize and leverage their giving. They know that however large their personal fortunes, they are dwarfed by the resources at the disposal of the public sector and the for-profit marketplace. To make a difference, they must concentrate their resources on problems not adequately dealt with by government or private businesses. In trying to help find solutions to some of the world's most intractable problems, they can take risks to find new solutions that innovative governments and for-profit firms can then adopt on a larger scale.

Tactics. The modern philanthropist speaks about social investments. The language is entrepreneurial, sprinkled with references to metrics, scalability, accountability, and leverage, emphasizing the importance of being strategic and achieving an impact. They come at a time when the idea of entrepreneurial solutions to social problems is gaining momentum.

By pioneering in the development of a hybrid philanthropy model, blending giving to nonprofit organizations and investing in for-profit businesses, the tech billionaires, who reaped the benefits of capitalism, led by Pierre M. Omidyar, the founder of eBay, Stephen M. Case, the former CEO of America Online and ex-chairman of AOL Time Warner, and Sergey Brin and Larry Page, the cofounders of Google, believe it can be applied in the service of charity. Thus, they are impatient with longstanding lines drawn between business and philanthropy by legal, regulatory, and tax regimes.

They often search for both nonprofit entities and for-profit social purpose businesses, the latter combining both enterprise and social good. They seek to integrate the private sector, which is oriented to making money and the social sector, which is focused on serving society. According to Case, "We can and should integrate these concepts and these missions. Instead of all the organizations tending toward the extremes, the most dynamic, innovative zone would be somewhere in the middle, with businesses that are not only for-profit and social-service groups with their own earned income all contributing to positive, durable, meaningful social change."[3]

Looking beyond the traditional approaches of private foundations as the exclusive vehicle for philanthropic initiatives, Omidyar, Skoll, Case, Brin, and Page are impatient individuals. They have accumulated vast wealth and are motivated to solve the immense, seemingly interdependent global problems of poverty, disease, and environmental degradation. Wanting to implement a high-impact strategy,[4] they are troubled by the inadequate efforts of the national and transnational public sector to ameliorate these problems. They are pioneering in the development of new partnerships between and among the nonprofit, for-profit, and public sectors. With the existence of massive pools of wealth, they exemplify the effort to put their assets to work to meet social needs and solve societal problems, but with a hybridization of means. These innovators often use a market orientation with the objective to generate a social benefit.

A great rivalry exists among the new philanthropists, perhaps more now intense than even the competition among for-profit businesses. Billionaires try to outdo each other not only in how much they give away, but also how effective they can be in tackling social problems, through a variety of means. They are striving to develop a compassionate capitalism of doing well, by doing good. However, compared with the resources of the public and private sectors, their philanthropic capital and their annual grants are still tiny.

Overview of the Book

After discussing the rise of the grant-giving megafoundations pioneered by Carnegie and Rockefeller in Chapter 2, chapter three focuses on the wealthiest and most prominent tech billionaire, William H. (Bill) Gates Jr. In 1999, Gates and his wife merged two existing family foundations, creating the Bill & Melinda Gates Foundation, the world's largest private foundation. The Gateses, now joined by billionaire-investor extraordinaire Warren E. Buffett, have followed a more traditional path delineated by Carnegie and Rockefeller, thinking big and focusing on clear goals. Using its massive resources and embracing risk, but not knowing how the projects it funds will turn out, the Gates Foundation seeks a long-term cure for, not just the treatment of the symptoms of, social ills, including K-12 public education in the United States and public health in the world's poorest nations. Looking for gaps in giving as well as areas of public and private sector inactivity, in the field of, for example, global health inequities, the foundation focuses on trying to solve problems where no one else has previously stepped in. Bill Gates has also used his personal leadership and presence to call attention to issues of significance to him.

Ebay's Pierre Omidyar and Jeffrey Skoll, discussed in Chapter 4 and 5, respectively, have pioneered a culture of giving among Silicon Valley's new money types. Seeing the traditional foundation model, as implemented by Gates on a massive scale, as too hidebound, they have brought a venture capitalist mindset to the business of philanthropy. Each in his own way is blazing a new trail.

Omidyar has sought to blur the lines between business and philanthropy. Omidyar Network serves as an innovative model for hybrid philanthropy. Including both a tax exempt arm and a taxpaying investment vehicle, it funds both nonprofit entities and for-profit social purpose businesses in an effort to create opportunities for individuals to make a difference and help people make a better life for themselves and for their communities. Few efforts blur the line between making money and doing good as do the for-profit microfinance organizations, backed by the Omidyar Network and the Tufts-Omidyar Microfinance Fund, which provide small loans to poor people starting or expanding their own businesses.

The Skoll Foundation funds projects undertaken by social entrepreneurs who apply businesslike approaches to solving social problems. Skoll sees the need for longer-term funding than foundations typically have offered, emphasizing the sustainability of supported organizations, permitting grantees more flexibility in spending funds, and partnering with recipients in thinking about how to measure success and helping in getting their message out to a wider audience. He focuses on a method, social entrepreneurship as undertaken by nonprofit organizations, not program areas, such as health or education, or narrow interests, such as healthcare for children. Skoll seeks to identify the most promising social entrepreneurs, individuals with innovative ideas that address pressing social problems and generate a public benefit, and then to amplify their impact. He also funded and led a for-profit film production venture to spread the word directly on causes he supports through filmanthropy—films with a social message.

Though his innovative, but much smaller, private foundation, which seeks to merge the distinctions between charity and the public and private sectors, Steve Case, as discussed in Chapter 6, has become a big proponent of hybrid philanthropy. More importantly, Case is a proponent of creating and building mission-driven for-profit businesses. He funded the Revolution Group LLC, which seeks to invest in companies giving consumers more choice and control over healthcare, through its web-based healthcare information service, among other endeavors.

Sergey Brin and Larry Page created *Google.org*, the philanthropic unit of Google Inc. As analyzed in Chapter 7, the Google arm includes a traditional tax exempt foundation that makes grants to nonprofits. *Google.org* also has the flexibility to invest in profit-making, but not necessarily profit-maximizing, ventures that also generate significant social and environmental returns. Building on Google Inc.'s information management and engineering prowess, Brin and Page are pioneering in creating a brand-enhancing, profit-making, taxpaying type of philanthropy designed to tackle systemic problems, including alleviating climate change by developing more advanced hybrid cars and finding renewable energy sources that are less expensive than coal, creating systems to predict and prevent disease pandemics, and empowering the poor with information about public services. *Google.org* also seeks to create jobs by investing in small and medium-size businesses in the developing world.

The book concludes in Chapter 8 with a discussion of the value added by the new philanthropists. It examines their impact on older and other contemporary philanthropists, both of whom also dedicated themselves to a quest for a better world. After assessing Bill Gates' call for a revision of capitalism, what he calls "creative capitalism," it provides a brief overview of Muhammud Yunus's concept of social enterprises, a hybrid business form, hopefully combining the best features of the for-profit sector with the best aspects of the nonprofit sector. Also considered are the possibilities offered by a social stock market, which may help overcome the lack of access to capital needed to build sustainable social enterprises to scale.

The transformation of philanthropy, in which the lines blur between the for-profit and nonprofit sectors, between business and philanthropy, marks the growing engagement in charitable giving by the tech billionaires profiled in this book. More generally, the tech billionaires may spur the development of hybrid business forms and the ability to link donors and investors with social purpose entities. It may be possible to both make money and do good. We may be on the verge of finding creative solutions to seemingly intractable social and environmental problems.

Before analyzing the impact of the new philanthropists, we first consider the founders of modern private foundations in the United States, Andrew Carnegie and John D. Rockefeller Sr.

Notes

1. Luisa Kroll with Matthew Miller, "Billionaires 2008," *Forbes* 181:6 ()March 24, 2008)80-160.
2. Patrick Goldstein, "Merging Movies and Activism," *Los Angeles Times*, November 15, 2005, E1. See also *BusinessWeek*, "Jeffrey Skoll: Why Delay? Give It Away" 3860 (December 1, 2003): 84.
3. Nicole Wallace, "Blending Business and Charity," *Chronicle of Philanthropy* 18:24 (September 28, 2006): 14-15, at 14.
4. Katie Hafner, "With Sudden Wealth, the Desire for Sudden Impact," *New York Times*, November 12, 2007, H28.

2

Private Foundations in the United States: The Impact of Andrew Carnegie and John D. Rockefeller Sr.

Having made their fortunes during the industrial revolution in the nineteenth century, the philanthropists of the first golden age of giving formed the first big foundations. About one century ago, Andrew Carnegie and John D. Rockefeller Sr. set about, each in his own way, to modernize American society. Over the years, hugely wealthy Americans, such as Bill Gates and Warren E. Buffett, considered in Chapter 3, broadly followed the blueprint delineated by Andrew Carnegie in his 1889 essay, "The Gospel of Wealth."[1] Before discussing the impact of Carnegie and Rockefeller, this chapter presents a brief statistical overview of the current state of private foundations in the United States.

Some Statistics on Private Foundations in the United States

At the end of 2005, there were 71,000 foundations in United States. They controlled over one half trillion dollars in assets and made grants of $36.4 billion in 2005. Private giving by foundations rose to some $40.7 billion in 2006.[2]

Foundation assets are concentrated in relatively few entities. Two percent of U.S. private foundations control roughly 70 percent of all foundation assets.[3]

Assets have long served as the yardstick by which influence is measured in the foundation universe. In mid-2007, some fifty-four U.S. foundations had assets in excess of $1 billion.[4] The Gates Foundation, discussed in Chapter 3, ranked first with more than $33 billion in assets, followed by the Ford Foundation ($11.6 billion), J. Paul Getty Trust ($9.6 million), Robert Wood Johnson Foundation ($9.3 billion), William and Flora Hewlett Foundation ($8.2 billion), Lilly Endowment Inc. ($8.3

billion), and W.K. Kellogg Foundation ($7.8 billion). The venerable Rockefeller Foundation was number thirteen in the pecking order with $3.4 billion in assets; the Carnegie Corporation of New York with a mere $2.5 billion came in at number nineteen.

Carnegie and Rockefeller: The Beginnings of Megaphilanthropy in the United States

The pairing of Bill Gates and Warren E. Buffett in 2006, discussed in the next chapter, invite comparison to Andrew Carnegie and John D. Rockefeller Sr. Carnegie and Rockefeller, as the wealthiest men in the United States at the turn of the twentieth century, separately embarked on huge philanthropic endeavors. As pioneers in big business each made second careers out of philanthropy, giving away hundreds of millions of dollars in the last decades of their respective lives after they made their mark in commerce. Each endowed a foundation, the Carnegie Corporation of New York and the Rockefeller Foundation, still in existence.

Carnegie's Approach to Philanthropy

About 120 years ago, Andrew Carnegie asserted in his 1889 "Gospel of Wealth" essay that all personal wealth beyond a family's moderate needs ought to be regarded as a trust fund for the community's benefit. For Carnegie, the community, not any individual no matter how talented and hard working, was the source of wealth. Thus, to the community dollars ought to be returned. The money should be given, he believed, during the benefactor's lifetime to ensure it would accomplish the maximum good.

Growing economic inequality, Carnegie believed as a good Social Darwinian, was the inescapable source, the wealth-creation that made social progress possible. To prevent this inequality from undoing the "ties of brotherhood" that "bind together the rich and poor in harmonious relationship," he argued that the wealthy had a duty to devote their fortunes to philanthropy. Not to do so represented the worst sort of personal failures because, as he put it, "The man who dies rich thus dies disgraced."[5]

Despite Carnegie's lofty sentiments in 1889, questions about his fortune multiplied over the years, especially after the summer of 1892, when armed Pinkerton guards intervened to break a strike at his Homestead steel mill, blackening his reputation.[6] Carnegie asserted that he kept wages low to remain competitive. Lower labor costs led, of course, to higher profits. In his view, it was better for him to squeeze money from employees' paychecks, accumulate it, and give back to the community, during his lifetime.

Making the dispersion of his fortune his credo after he sold his steel company in 1901, Carnegie's determination became a career, during the last eighteen years of his life (1901-1919). He sought to make the process as rational as possible, applying the same organizational skills to giving away funds as he used to amass his wealth.

As a self-made man, he created not only a huge, powerful corporate empire but also a vast personal fortune. His personal history impacted his giving.

Carnegie sought to equip the public with the skills needed to escape poverty, in other words, to empower them. To uplift humanity, he saw the building of libraries as the best way to reach the broadest group of people. With libraries as his first charitable focus, Carnegie built some 2,507 libraries worldwide, including 1,681 in the United States, at a cost in excess of $56 million (several billion dollars today), so that the illiterate could learn to read.[7] Carnegie built these libraries on condition that the municipalities stock them with books and maintain them, thereby forcing the public sector to participate in providing an essential service.

Prior to his death, Carnegie's philanthropic efforts expanded beyond libraries. In 1905, he created what became known as the Carnegie Foundation for the Advancement of Teaching, followed by the Carnegie Endowment for International Peace in 1910. In 1911-1912, he transferred the bulk of his remaining fortune, $125 million, to the first megafoundation, the Carnegie Corporation of New York.[8]

Although Carnegie gave away 90 percent of his fortune during his lifetime, more than $350 million, he left it to others manage his philanthropy after his death under the Carnegie Corporation's vague rubric: to promote "the advancement and diffusion of knowledge among the people of the United States...."[9] In refusing to hold his foundation a hostage to the past, he went further stating: "...I give my Trustees full authority to change policy or causes hitherto aided, from time to time, when this, in their opinion, has become necessary or desirable."[10]

Rockefeller's Approach to Philanthropy

Even more than Carnegie, the oil baron John D. Rockefeller Sr. transformed philanthropy into a business. On walking way from directing Standard Oil in 1896, he was the richest person of his time and reviled as a greedy monopolist. In 1906, the federal government targeted the Standard Oil empire under the antitrust laws. The litigation culminated in 1911 with United States Supreme Court ordering the dismemberment of Standard Oil.[11]

Carving out his own sectors of philanthropic interest,[12] Rockefeller used his fortune to identify and attack important public health problems in the United States, a theme emphasized globally by Bill Gates in the twenty-first century. Rockefeller promoted medical research, especially where the findings could lead to broad social benefits, such as eliminating the rural South of hookworm.

He also built educational institutions from scratch. In 1901, he endowed the Rockefeller Institute for Medical Research (now the Rockefeller University), the first major educational institution devoted to medical research, and dedicated it to discovering the causes, prevention and cure of diseases. He previously had founded and sustained the University of Chicago and in 1902 funded the General Education Board, which first promoted the education of blacks and later medical education. He also raised the standards of medical education by giving funds to medical schools that used the Johns Hopkins Medical School as a model.

In 1913, he established the Rockefeller Foundation, which he endowed with $183 million. From 1889 until his death in 1937, Rockefeller gave away some $530 million.[13]

The Impact of Megafoundations and Their Current Transformation

From Carnegie and Rockefeller onward, although some commentators felt that foundations overwhelmingly devoted their expenditures to preserving the status quo,[14] many megafoundations, particularly over the last forty years or so, dedicated themselves to a quest for a better world. They sought solutions to underlying social problems that previously had resisted intellect and money, focusing not only on their own efforts but also facilitating and enhancing the public sector's ability to solve important societal ills through social engineering. The scientific philanthropy pioneered by Carnegie and Rockefeller searched for the root causes of human distress—whether economic, social, or physical—and sought to spur the development of innovative solutions to these pressing social difficulties.[15] In other words, they attempted to cure societal problems at the source, whether illiteracy, the distress brought about by poor health and ultimately death, and more recently, social and economic inequality, rather than merely treating the symptoms.

Prodded by the Gates Foundation, to which we next turn, changes recently have occurred among many megafoundations, a topic considered in Chapter 8. The Gates Foundation's immense assets offer the possibility of doing enormous good in preventing and battling diseases in the Third World, among other areas of interest.

Notes

1. Andrew Carnegie, *The Gospel of Wealth and Other Timely Essays*, ed. Edward C. Kirkland (Cambridge: Belknap Press of Harvard University Press, 1962); Andrew Carnegie, "The Gospel of Wealth," in *The Responsibilities of Wealth*, ed. Dwight F. Burlingame (Bloomington, IN: Indiana University Press, 1992).
2. The statistics in this paragraph are from Foundation Center, "Highlights of Foundation Yearbook," 2007 Edition <*http://foundation.org/gainknowledge/research/pdf/fy2007-highlights.pdf*>. See also Stephanie Strom, "Foundations' Giving Is Said To Have Set Record in '06," *New York Times*, April 13, 2007, A15.
3. Joel L. Fleishman, *The Foundation: A Great American Secret—How Private Wealth Is Changing the World* (New York: PublicAffairs, 2007), 27.
4. Foundation Center, "Top Funders: Top 100 U.S. Foundations by Asset Size" <*http://foundationcenter.org/findfunders/topfunders/top100assets.html*> (July 9, 2007). See also Fleishman, *Foundation*, 267.
5. The quotations in this paragraph are from Carnegie, *Gospel of Wealth*, 14, 29, 30 (1962 edition).
6. The Homestead tragedy is recounted in Peter Krass, *Carnegie* (Hoboken, NJ: John Wiley, 2002), 275-303. See also David Nasaw, *Andrew Carnegie* (New York: Penguin, 2006), 405-427, 430-448.
7. Robert M. Lester, *Forty Years of Carnegie Giving* (New York: Charles Scribner's Sons, 1941), 92-93. See also Nasaw, *Carnegie*, 607; Joseph Frazier Wall, *Andrew Carnegie* (New York: Oxford University Press, 1970) 828-829, n.1, 1101.
8. Lester, *Forty Years*, 45-63. See also Nasaw, *Carnegie*, 671, 742, 766; Wall, *Carnegie*, 871, 873, 882-883; Krass, *Carnegie*, 503. See generally, Maury Klein, *The Change Makers: From Carnegie to Gates, How the Great Entrepreneurs Transformed Ideas into Industries* (New York: Times Books, 2003), 247-248.
9. Carnegie Corporation of New York, "The Corporation's Program" <*http:www.carnegie.org/sub/program/areas.html*> (September 19, 2007). See also Nasaw, *Carnegie*, 767; Wall, *Carnegie*, 883.
10. "New Directions for Carnegie Corporation of New York: A Report to the Board by Vartan Gregorian, President, February 2, 1999 <*http:www.carnegie.org/sub/program/ndpage1.html*> (September 19, 2007). See also Vartan Gregorian, "The Charity Chain," *Forbes* 179:10 (May 7, 2007): 240-241, at 240.
11. Standard Oil Co. v. United States, 221 US 1 (1911).
12. Ron Chernow, *Titan: The Life of John D. Rockefeller, Sr.* (New York: Random House, 1998), 302-320, 323-329, 472-479, 483-493. See generally Raymond B. Fosdick, *The Story of the Rockefeller Foundation* (New York: Harper, 1952), reprinted (New Brunswick, NJ: Transaction Publishers, 1989) and Klein, *Change Makers*, 248-249.
13. Chernow, *Titan*, 566, 568-569, 570.
14. See, e.g., Eduard C. Lindeman, *Wealth and Culture: A Study of One Hundred Foundations and Community Trusts and Their Operations During the Decade 1921-1930* (New Brunswick, NJ: Transaction Publishers, 1988).
15. Fleishman, *Foundation*, 39-43.

3

Bill and Melinda Gates Foundation: Big Goals but Following the Traditional Foundation Model

In the mid-1970s, William H. (Bill) Gates Jr., along with his business partner, Paul G. Allen, founded Microsoft, a company that would revolutionize home computer systems and make Gates the richest man in the world. Through its MS-DOS program and Windows operating system, Microsoft made computers accessible to the average person, allowing users to perform an amazing array of tasks. Microsoft's influence can be gauged not just by looking at the programs it has created over the years, but by the sheer wealth it has generated. Microsoft has made billionaires out of four people and it is estimated another 10,000 employees millionaires by 2000 through their stock holdings.[1]

In recent years, Bill and his wife, Melinda French Gates, have taken their vast wealth into the world of philanthropy, creating the world's largest foundation. Similar to Carnegie and Rockefeller's philanthropic efforts, the Gates Foundation is attacking the root causes of social problems, focusing particularly on healthcare in developing nations.[2] Its programs span the globe, from healthcare and poverty alleviation in Third World countries, to public school innovation in the United States and even smaller, local initiatives in the Pacific Northwest.

Perhaps the biggest news in the world of philanthropy in the first decade of the twenty-first century was the announcement in June 2006 by Warren E. Buffett, the CEO of Berkshire Hathaway, Inc. that over a period of years he would contribute the bulk of his vast fortune to the Bill & Melinda Gates Foundation, which will more than double its annual funding. What this newfound wealth will allow the Gates Foundation to accomplish remains to be seen, but what is certain, Bill and Melinda Gates now have the power to change the fortunes of the poorer countries of the world to a degree exceeded only by the wealthiest industrialized nations.

Background on Bill Gates

Bill Gates was born in 1955, the son of a successful attorney and a schoolteacher. A Harvard dropout, he teamed up with a Seattle schoolmate, Paul Allen, to write the first computer program for a personal computer and then to co-found Microsoft in 1975.[3] At the time, personal computers were the realm of hobbyists who were accustomed to using free software. As a result, Gates and Allen's program, BASIC, was pirated early on. Gates then decided to try to change the prevailing trend, arguing that high quality programming software could not be given away free of charge.

From these humble roots the Microsoft empire rose. Gates was one of the first to spot the value of splitting software and operating systems from the hardware. He had the foresight to understand the importance of owning the dominant operating system in the emerging information technology industry, and he constantly pushed for advances and improvements in Microsoft's offerings in this field.

But it was not until Microsoft's partnership with IBM that the company took off. The computer giant needed an operating system and Gates knew of one that had been developed by a fellow Seattle technology pioneer, Tim Patterson, of Seattle Computer Products. The program's name was DOS. Gates approached Patterson and the two agreed on a deal whereby Microsoft would become the exclusive licensing agent of DOS and would eventually get full ownership. Microsoft began to aggressively market the DOS program, which it renamed MS-DOS (Microsoft-Disc Operating System), and the firm soon became the leader in software technology.

Gates became America's wealthiest person in 1995, when his fortune topped $18 billion.[4] By 2006 even after his vast philanthropic donations, which began in 1994, Forbes estimated his net worth at $53 billion.[5] For the thirteenth year in a row the 2007 *Forbes* survey of the world's billionaires, ranked him at number one, with a net worth of $56 billion; Gates fell to number three in 2008, with a net worth of $58 billion.[6] In 2000, Gates stepped down as CEO of Microsoft, becoming its chairman of its board of directors and chief software architect. In 2008, he stepped aside from Microsoft, remaining only as chairman, and devoted most of his time to the Gates Foundation.

The Gates Foundation

Growing up, Bill Gates was taught by his late mother that he had a responsibility to give back. On the eve of Bill and Melinda's wedding in January 1994, Gates's mother, ill from cancer, wrote a letter to Bill's fiancée, Melinda French, stressing the opportunities the couple would have to improve the world and the responsibilities that came with their enormous wealth. She closed the letter: "From those to whom much is given, much is expected."[7] Melinda recalled, "It was really quite beautiful. And that was what got us going."[8] Besides his mother, seemingly Melinda directed more of Bill's attention to the world outside of Microsoft.

Bill and Melinda Gates created their first foundation, the William H. Gates Foundation, named after his father, in 1994. As Gates Sr. explained, "Undoubtedly part of the impetus was that Bill just had so much money. For years he talked about the fact that he was ultimately going to give it away. He's no dummy. He began to see that he didn't need to wait. In the early days he was an entrepreneur wanting to keep control of his company. Then that changed."[9]

As Gates Sr. retired from his law practice in 1994, he suggested that Bill establish a foundation he could run in consultation with his son. Thus the William H. Gates Foundation, which began in Gates Sr.'s basement, came to existence with a $94 million contribution from Gates Jr.

Three years later, in 1997, Bill and Melinda Gates created a second foundation, the Gates Library Foundation, subsequently renamed the Gates Learning Foundation.[10] Similar to Carnegie, the Gateses focused on libraries, but beyond Carnegie, they focused on wiring, not building, them to reduce the digital divide. The second foundation brought computers, Internet access, training, and technical support to libraries in low-income areas of the United States. From 1998 to 2004, this foundation (and its successor foundation) installed 47,000 computers in 11,000 U.S. public libraries.[11] Bringing technologies to libraries remains an interest of the Gateses today through their foundation's U.S. Program and its Global Development Program.

Then in August 1999, the Gateses announced that they would combine the two foundations into the Bill & Melinda Gates Foundation. The new entity was officially created in 2000, with its assets increased to $17 billion.[12] According to the foundation's website, the values that lie at the core of the foundation's work are: "All lives—no matter where they are being led—have equal value" and, reflecting Bill's mother's admonition, "To whom much is given, much is expected."[13] As Bill Gates subsequently reflected:

> It's hard to escape the conclusion that in our world, some lives are seen as worth saving, but others are not. And that realization really forced us not only to start our philanthropy earlier but also to make reducing inequity the central priority of our giving.
>
> We want the world to allocate its resources knowing that the death of a child in a poor country is every bit as tragic as that of a child in a rich country. The principle that every human life has equal worth guides us to look for the most effective ways to reduce that suffering that comes as a result of inequity. To us, that means improving economic opportunity and health in developing countries, as well as education in the United States.[14]

With a reputation as a brilliant, but ruthless, businessman, Bill Gates' philanthropy perhaps served an ulterior motive in 1999. It may have been, in part, an effort to burnish his public image in light of the U.S. government's high profile antitrust suit brought against Microsoft in May 1998, which alleged that Microsoft engaged in anticompetitive behavior.[15] A federal district court judge issued findings of fact in November 1999 and conclusion of law in June 2000, which were affirmed by a federal court of appeals in June 2001, that the firm had engaged in monopolization violations of the Sherman Antitrust Act.[16] The case was settled in November 2001 with Microsoft making some concessions.[17] The terms of the settlement were quite technical and are beyond the scope of this book. However, nearly a decade later, few doubt the sincerity of Bill and Melinda Gates in their philanthropic endeavors.

Tax and Other Benefits of a Private Foundation

Income, gift, and estate tax savings also may have influenced Bill Gates to form a foundation. Donors to private foundations and the entities themselves receive preferential tax treatment. Donors who contribute long-term appreciated stock to foundations, such as Gates' Microsoft shares, are not subject to capital gains taxation—that is, the profit they make on the shares is not taxable. They also receive a deduction for federal income tax purposes.[18] In brief, they can deduct the full, fair market value of their gifted, publicly traded stock up to 20 percent of their adjusted gross income if given to most private foundations, subject to a limited carryover provision that allows them to take deductions in subsequent years if they could not fully use the deduction on funding the foundation. This fair market value deduction for gifts of qualified appreciated stock, that is, publicly traded stock that is capital gain property, only applies, however, if the donor's total gifts of such stock do not exceed 10 percent of the value of all of the corporation's outstanding shares. For amounts in excess of 10 percent, the charitable donation decreases to the donor's cost (more technically, his or her basis) for the shares. Furthermore, the federal gift tax is not imposed on charitable contributions for the fair market value of contributions to private foundations.[19] Also, the gifted shares are removed from a donor's estate.

Apart from a 2 percent (or in some cases, 1 percent) excise tax on net investment income, private foundations, generally speaking, are not subject to federal taxation, apart from the imposition of certain excise taxes discussed later in this chapter.

Under federal and state law, donors and foundations possess broad freedom to define their purposes and further them. For instance, Washington State law permits the creation of a general purpose, perpetual organization, such as a trust, dedicated to serving an indefinite class of beneficiaries.[20] As a charitable trust under Washington State law, the Gates Foundation is subject to the scrutiny of the Washington Attorney General, who, as a practical matter, only polices egregious violations of state law. Federal responsibility for oversight of foundations rests with the Tax Exempt & Government Entities Division of the Internal Revenue Service, a unit with "resources inadequate to the task."[21]

Buffett's Impact

Despite having given away more money more quickly than any entity in history, by the end of 2005, the foundation's endowment reached $29 billion, dwarfing other philanthropic organizations.[22] Then in June 2006, Warren E. Buffett, the celebrated billionaire investor, announced he would contribute roughly 85 percent of his Berkshire Hathaway fortune to charity, with five sixths of it going to the Gates Foundation.[23]

By putting aside his ego, Buffett's contribution is remarkable, reflecting the longstanding desire of philanthropists, going back to Carnegie and Rockefeller, to leave a lasting, personal imprint through the creation of a foundation in their own name. However, following his own investment model, Buffett endorsed the Gateses' philanthropic ideas. In backing the Gateses, he put his assets in the hands of a good organization with talented (and trusted) managers and gave them the freedom to make decisions. On announcing his gift, Buffett stated, "You need to seek out people with a talent to distribute money in the same way as you do for those to accumulate it."[24] Believing that the Gateses could do philanthropy better than he could, Buffett realized there was an established foundation with staff and programs in place, that could productively use his money now and in coming years, before his death. Buffett planned to transfer some $31 billion (as of June 2006) of his shares in Berkshire Hathaway, Inc., an insurance holding company that serves as his investment vehicle, in increments over many years. He made the first transfer of 500,000 shares, worth roughly $1.6 billion in August 2006.

Under the terms of his gift, beginning in 2009, Buffett required the foundation to spend in the current year the value of the shares he gave it in the previous year. Thus, the foundation will double its annual spending to approximately $3.5 billion, depending on the value of the Berkshire stock, to reflect the size of Buffett's gifts, with annually one out of every ten U.S. foundation dollars having the Gates' name on its. By mandating this yearly distribution of his gifts, Buffett magnified the foundation's impact and guaranteed that assets will not accumulate in the Gates Foundation. Additionally, his money in the form of annual contributions will flow to the foundation only as long as either Bill or Melinda remains active in the policy-setting and administration of the foundation. If Buffett dies before the transfer of all the shares designated for the foundation, the balance will go at once to the foundation, provided Bill or Melinda remains involved in the foundation.

The years following Buffett's commitment brought new challenges. It stretched the organization as it struggled to cope with a sharp increase in demands for support beyond not only its existing administrative capacity but also its strategic objectives. Higher visibility triggered calls to bring the foundation's investment policies more in line with its stated goals through a mission-related investment program. However, in response to its critics, the foundation initially expressed skepticism about the mission-related investment concept, maintaining it strives to maximum financial returns to increase the funds available to further its philanthropic goals. However, the Gateses instructed their managers to vote shareholder proxies consistent with the principles of good governance and good management and to consider issues beyond corporate profits, including the foundation's values, in making investment decisions. The only explicitly banned actions are purchasing shares of tobacco companies and firms with links to the Sudan.[25]

The Gates Foundation Today

The Bill & Melinda Gates Foundation follows the traditional institutional structure of large-scale philanthropy. Following the Carnegie and Rockefeller models, the founders of modern philanthropy, detailed in Chapter 2, Bill Gates set up a private foundation to realize his and Melinda's goals. He initially established a trust as a perpetual entity with an expansive statement of purpose. However, if Bill Gates does not serve as a trustee and in any event on his death, the foundation's purposes are "limited to those consistent with the charitable goals and directions that I [Bill Gates] have set forth in my lifetime, including without limitation, providing access to technology, world health and population solutions, education and charitable giving in the Northwestern part of the United States."[26]

After Buffett's gift and in response to its critics, in October 2006, the Gates Foundation separated its program work from its investment activities. It also decided to spend down its assets within fifty years after Bill's and Melinda's deaths. As restructured the foundation consists of two entities: the Bill & Melinda Gates Foundation Asset Trust, which invests the foundation's endowment, and a programmatic foundation, which spends the endowment. The trust, including annual installments of Buffett's gifts, funds the programmatic foundation. Bill and Melinda Gates serve as the sole trustees of the trust's assets. The second entity, the Bill & Melinda Gates Foundation, conducts the foundation's programmatic and grant-making activities. It has three trustees, Bill and Melinda Gates and Warren Buffet.[27] Buffett, as the third trustee of the programmatic foundation, basically views his role as a custodian if Bill and Melinda were both to die in an accident. Following a common organizational model, it has co-CEOs, one of whom is Gates Sr. It employs a full-time staff who handle day-to-day management.

With its enormous resources and a broad statement of purpose, the foundation faced the task of defining its areas of interest. "[W]e concentrate on a few areas of giving so we can learn about the best approaches and have the greatest possible impact," Bill and Melinda wrote. "We choose these issues by asking: which problems affect the most people, and which have been neglected in the past?"[28]

Inequity is of particular concern to Bill Gates, perhaps out of a sense of guilt, if not nobility of purpose. As he stated in early 2007:

> It's hard to escape the conclusion that in our world, some lives are seen as worth saving, but others are not. And that realization really forced us not only to start our philanthropy earlier but also to make reducing inequity the central priority of our giving.[29]

In delivering the commencement address to the Harvard University class of 2007, he further noted: "But humanity's greatest advances are not in its discoveries—but in how those discoveries are applied to reduce inequity. Whether through democracy, strong public education, quality health care, or broad economic opportunity—reducing inequity is the highest human achievement."[30] Noble sentiments, but perhaps unattainable in practice.

Reflecting its commitment to reduce some of the world's most challenging inequities by addressing the root causes of selected social problems, the foundation today focuses on three programmatic areas: a United States Program, a Global Health Program, and a Global Development Program, each managed by a president. Responding to criticism that the foundation is unaccountable to anyone beyond the Gateses, each of the three divisions has an advisory board, consisting of six luminaries, appointed for a single three-year term. Each advisory board meets twice a year.

The *United States Program* has sought to improve public high schools nationwide, thereby increasing the number of high school graduates who possess the skills needed to succeed in college and at work. Initially focusing on creating smaller schools out of larger ones, its $1 billion effort to redesign high schools includes not only redesigning the schools themselves, in terms of structure and size, but also revamping curriculum and instruction.[31] Rather than creating and building educational institutions, as Rockefeller did, the Gates Foundation gives money to existing public school systems and charter schools.[32]

Its largest grant-making program, the *Global Health Program*, seeks to tackle and redress global health inequities, particularly in the developing world, in six areas: infectious diseases, HIV/AIDS, tuberculosis, reproductive health, global health strategies, and global health technologies, as well as research, advocacy and policy endeavors.[33]

Examining global public health concerns and realizing that preventable diseases, such as malaria, were killing millions or people each year stunned Bill and Melinda Gates in the 1990s. They sought to solve problems where no one else had stepped in. According to Bill Gates:

> We couldn't even believe it. You think in philanthropy that your dollars will just be marginal, because the really juicy obvious things will all have been taken. So you look at this stuff and we are, like, *wow*! When somebody is saying to you we can save many lives for hundreds of dollars each, the answer has to be no, no, no. That would already have been done. We go to events where people are raising money for various illnesses where lives are being treated as if they were worth millions of dollars. And here we were learning that you can save even more lives for a few hundred each. We really did think it was too shocking to be true.[34]

Evidencing a faith in human progress, the foundation's healthcare efforts reflect Bill's belief in the power of science and technology to change (and improve) lives and thus reduce inequalities of opportunity. Reflecting this technological approach can surmount problems that seem insurmountable, he stated, "Technology is a central focus of our foundation partly because it can help us see what's really going on in the world." He continued, "Just as technology allows us to see the world's inequities, it can also help us address them."[35]

The foundation has taken the lead in stimulating research into global health, bringing attention and resources to diseases, such as malaria and tuberculosis, long neglected by pharmaceutical firms and scientists because they are concentrated in the developing world. It focuses its funding on: research to develop effective, affordable, and practical health solutions; increasing access to vaccines, drugs, and other tools to fight diseases prevalent in the developing world; and advocacy to bring new interest and funders to support the work it does.[36]

The foundation has poured billions of dollars into cutting-edge scientific research grants focused on preventing, treating, and curing neglected diseases of the developing world, such as malaria, HIV/AIDS, and tuberculosis. If successful, these funds would save future lives. Its approach focuses on a long-term process, viewing as a realistic possibility the overcoming of global health problems, particularly certain diseases long banished from the developed world, through research. Following this long-term approach, its grants enable researchers to avoid the uncertainty inherent in the traditional year-to-year funding of grants or the unpredictability of governmental funding. Again, rather than creating and building health organizations, the foundation generally works with established entities, identifying successful projects that are underway.

In striving to harness science to tackle some of the Third World's most intractable health problems and thereby improve health in the developing nations, its lofty ambitions include funding research for the development of vaccines and drugs for malaria, HIV/AIDS, and tuberculosis. It takes on these risky projects, hoping for scientific and technological breakthroughs, in contrast to supporting basic healthcare. For example, through the $450 million Grand Challenges in Global Health Initiative, which it largely funded, the foundation sought to jumpstart numerous, sometimes exotic, biomedical research projects designed to help the world's poorest people. The project focuses on fourteen research areas consisting of a series of obstacles to progress, and which, if solved, could lead to dramatic improvements in global health.[37] Although retaining marketing rights in developed nations, the Initiative's grantees pledged to make their discoveries available at little or no cost to developing countries.

In 2007, the foundation unveiled a new initiative, the Grand Challenge Explorations, an expansion of its commitment to the Grand Challenges in Global Health Initiative. The new program will support hundreds of early-stage medical research projects with $100,000 grants. It will encourage the best and brightest to take risks on novel ideas.[38]

The Gateses view the foundation's resources and rigor as a catalyst for researchers who are inventing new tools or may achieve medical breakthroughs that are effective, inexpensive to produce and thus affordable, easy to distribute and simple to use, thereby saving the lives of millions of people. Reflecting an entrepreneurial approach and trying to egg on drug companies to work on vaccines for the Third World, according to Bill, "This is a magic time in terms of the momentum we can get going."[39]

As the largest single recipient of its largesse, the foundation has pledged a total of $1.5 billion in 1999 and 2005 to the Global Alliance for Vaccines and Immunization, now the GAVI Alliance (GAVI), to improve access to vaccines to fight diseases common in developing nations.[40] Started by the Gates Foundation, in conjunction with a diverse, innovative group of public and private partners, GAVI buys existing, routine vaccines and distributes them to the globe's poorest children. By having rich nations match the foundation's donations, these funds will provide market incentives to pharmaceutical firms to generate a supply of needed vaccines. Manufacturers respond knowing that if they ramp up production, there will be a buyer. GAVI guarantees the purchase of huge doses of vaccines to prevent Third World diseases. The partnership has helped save the lives of hundreds of thousands, if not millions, of children who received basic vaccines. As the vaccination programs proceeded, GAVI also turned its attention to counter the massive outflow of health workers from developing nations and to create a $500 million fund to improve general healthcare delivery, training, and immunization services.

In September 2005, five European nations pledged support for an innovative effort to expand GAVI's work. The new International Finance Facility for Immunization issued bonds against these countries' long-term aid commitments with the goal of raising up to $4 billion for GAVI. These bonds immediately unlocked the full value of the multi-year aid packages, thereby providing more predictable funding for immunization programs.[41]

The foundation also gives grants designed to control malaria, among other diseases, using existing prevention and treatment tools, such as mosquito nets. Thus, in addition to funding high-risk research projects, the foundation seeks to create products and systems that can be replicated, and thereby expanded in scale, at little additional cost.

Finally, in 2006, the foundation initiated its *Global Development Program*, focusing on promoting financial services for the poor and improving agricultural production, particularly helping small-scale farmers gain access to markets, as well as water and sanitation, in developing nations in an effort to reduce the inequities associated with poverty.[42] The foundation came to realize that improving global health care involves more than merely providing vaccines or drugs. Seeing health in its social, economic, and political context, people must have the material means to improve their lot in life. If the children get to age five, how will they thrive? They need clean water and food as well as access to a good education. Their parents need a livelihood.

Its Financial Services for the Poor initiative includes funds for microfinance organizations which provide small, unsecured loans to help those living in poverty, mostly women, start (or expand) small businesses. These income-generating activities enable them to earn a livelihood and better provide for themselves and their families with life's basic necessities.

Microlending and Microfinance

Over the past thirty years, specialized, nongovernmental financial institutions have evolved to meet the capital needs of microentrepreneurs.[43] Today, some ten thousand microcredit organizations (MCOs) and microfinance organizations (MFOs), large and small, exist in 130 countries, offering upwards of 100 million borrowers the chance to start (or build) a business, with small loans, often a few hundred dollars or less, and accumulate capital.

The microcredit system does not depend on collateral or contracts. Following the widely replicated Grameen Bank model, pioneered by Dr. Muhammad Yunus, the winner of the 2006 Nobel Peace Prize, where a representative of the financial institution comes to the borrowers, MCOs lend to three- to nine-member groups, typically consisting of women. These so-called lending circles act as guarantors for each other. Peer support and pressure facilitate the repayment of loans as do bite-sized, weekly installments and the presence of loan officers in the field who know their borrowers through regular contacts. As the loans are repaid, the lending cycle continues with good borrowers receiving larger loans. Conversely, each lending circle agrees to share the financial burden if one of its members defaults on a loan. Group meetings allow MCOs to provide education to group members and also encourage the sharing of effective business techniques. Repayment rates of 95 to 98 percent, generally in excess of the nonperforming loan levels of mainstream commercial banks, characterize microlending.[44] However, the repayment rates may be overstated. New loans may allow borrowers to keep current on old loans. Individuals may borrow from one MCO to pay another, or from local moneylenders.[45]

Small loans, on the worldwide average of $250, help shift microenterprises toward sustainability and away from survival. These loans increase borrowers' incomes, lift families out of poverty, and promote the growth and productivity of their businesses. Economic development through microcredit also leads to social development—more education for children; better healthcare, housing, and nutrition; and women's empowerment—and the building of networks within a community, enabling people to tackle other problems, such as environmental degradation.[46] However, some MCOs may fail to ensure that borrowers use loans to expand or start small businesses. Rather, some loans go for consumption or healthcare.[47]

Microfinance is the broader umbrella of financial services provided to the world's poor under which microcredit is one piece. Microfinance organizations supply an array of financial services to low-income households beyond loans to microenterprises. With a stable and increasing cash flow, microentrepreneurs start saving to build assets and for future consumption. Also needing insurance (health, life, crop) and an inexpensive means to transfer funds, they require access to banking and insurance services. Microfinance thus represents an orientation to the operation of more commercially-based financial institutions.

Most MCOs and MFOs, roughly 9,700 to 9,800 out of 10,000 are not currently sustainable in terms of financial self-sufficiency.[48] Most MCOs and MFOs generally operate without the interest and fees charged covering their operating costs, the cost of capital, and loan losses. Emphasizing outreach to the very poorest, they generally lack institutional viability apart from non-capital market funding through grants as well as various subsidies from governments, international and nongovernmental organizations and donations from private donors, such as foundations.

Beyond the problem of sustainability, a clash of worldviews exists with respect to the essential nature of MCOs and MFOs. Business-oriented managers regard their social mission-oriented counterparts as soft with respect to hard realities of achieving financial sustainability. Development-oriented managers have difficulty understanding the hard-nosed attitude of business-oriented managers, operating from a traditional business perspective, to the needs of the poor, especially the poorest of the poor.

A tension also exists over whether MCOs and MFOs should offer: financial services only; financial and basic business-related services (such as marketing, budgeting, inventory management); or integrate non-financial services into their programs. Seeing poverty as a more complex phenomenon, needing a holistic approach, involving not only capital needs but also a variety of other factors, including integrated credit and social services, some organizations offer health and nutrition education and even healthcare.

Dr. Rajiv J. Shah, who oversees the Gates initiative, stated that microfinance "can reach hundreds of millions of people, and do so in a way that helps them move out of poverty and that sustains over time."[49] He indicated that the Gates Foundation is giving grants, providing loans, and making program-related investments to reach its goal of moving hundreds of millions out of poverty. Shah noted, "But the goal is always that—it's not to get a return. That distinction is important, because Omidyar has taken a different approach."[50]

Pierre Omidyar, the founder of eBay, is one of the leading proponents of microfinance. However, he differs somewhat from Gates and others, such as Muhammad Yunus, the father of microfinance, in that he believes the greatest advantage of microfinance is its potential to become scalable and profitable. To that end, Omidyar, as discussed in the next chapter, concentrates his work in the microfinance sector promoting various types of sustainable MCOs and MFOs, including profit-making ones, rather than making donations merely to nonprofit entities. "For us," he stated, "it's not about alleviating poverty; it's about economic self-empowerment."[51]

The Gates Foundation Funds Microcredit Institutions

Two of Gates's grants, one to Pro Mujer and another to Unitus, illustrate the difference between its approach to MFOs and that of Pierre

Omidyar. Pro Mujer (Mujer is "woman" in Spanish), exemplifies the integrative, social mission approach, serving the poorest of the poor, who either lack any reliable income sources or who engage in unregistered businesses run out of their residences or on street corners, but who also need business-related and social service. Pro Mujer, a nonprofit, non-governmental organization, founded in Bolivia in 1990, has taken the lead in offering a multi-faceted, integrated program. Now operating as a network of microfinance institutions in Bolivia, Mexico, Nicaragua, Peru, and Argentina (the latter began operations in November 2005), serving some 140,000 borrowers, it not only provides small loans for its very poor female borrowers to initiate or expand microenterprises, but also offers business development and healthcare education. It uses the infrastructure provided by its lending and savings microfinance operations as the vehicle for cost-effective social service delivery, thereby reducing costs. Pro Mujer integrates financial services with business training healthcare education and health services (in Bolivia, Nicaragua, and Peru) in a financially sustainable way. At the end of 2005, its four established microfinance institutions were self-sufficient.[52]

In March 2006, the Gates Foundation awarded a $3.1 million five-year grant to Pro Mujer. The grant will enable the MFO to develop a wider range of loan products for specific types of clients. It will finance research focusing on how to meet the untapped demand from parts of the poorest segment of the microfinance market not reached or effectively served by traditional microfinance models. The products will be developed and rolled out in pilot projects to demonstrate their potential for replication, impact, and contribution to an MFO's financial sustainability.[53]

Continuing its poverty-alleviation focus helps Pro Mujer retain access to public sector grants and private donor funding, such as the Gates Foundation. Nonprofit status provides access to less costly capital than could be obtained through commercial borrowing and more flexibility to innovate. Aware that it must achieve greater scale and achieve the cost-effective delivery of services through a replication model, Pro Mujer remains open to experimentation to find ways to best serve the disadvantaged women, particularly who are not yet involved in economic activity.

In October 2006, the Gates Foundation announced a $1.5 million, three-year grant to Unitus, Inc. (Unitus), a hybrid nonprofit organization, part strategic consulting firm, part venture capital firm, and part investment bank. Unitus, which was started in 2000 by Mike Murray, a former Microsoft executive, helps MFOs accelerate their growth and ultimately convert to for-profit status, if they are not already for-profit entities.

Unitus aims to create a new business model to speed the development of microfinance by opening it up to investors, with the objective of raising a much larger pool of capital than from donations alone.

Unitus focuses on helping create large-scale, commercially sustainable MFOs.[54] These MFOs then can assist hundreds of thousands of additional clients to work their way out of poverty. Unitus provides funding and capacity-building consulting services, such as technical assistance, to high-potential, mainly small and mid-sized, MFOs, that have the vision to grow rapidly, the base from which to improve their outreach and services, and dramatically increase the number of clients they serve.

Unitus's grants to its MFO partners constitute specific investments in improving their operating capacity in various areas, such as management information systems, computer software and hardware, and human resources development. It often acts as a guarantor, helping its MFO partners leverage credit through local banks. Unitus calls this type of assistance "catalytic debt" because it enables MFOs to prove to commercial banks that they are healthy, stable, well-run institutions. By negotiating term-sheet specifics between its partners and banks, Unitus helps ensure that its MFO partners receive the funding needed to meet their growth targets. Its MFO partners include Pro Mujer Mexico, where Unitus provides both grants and loans.

Steering clear of the for-profit versus nonprofit controversy, the Gates' grant will help Unitus identify potential efficiency innovations in the microfinance business model. It will enable Unitus to identify, study, and test ways to increase the operational and financial efficiency of MFOs providing financial services to the poor, thereby enabling these organizations to expand their services, lower their costs, and reduce interest rates they charge borrowers. Efficiency enhancing measures to be studied include reducing operating costs and increasing employee productivity through, for example, better use of technology in recording payments, tracking loans, and sharing information among lenders.[55]

As discussed in Chapter 4, Unitus created a separate entity, Unitus Equity Fund L.P., an affiliated for-profit organization, to raise money from investors who expect a financial return matching venture capital averages. Its investors include the Omidyar Network, but not the Gates Foundation.

The Gates Foundation: An Assessment

Although vast in size, and getting bigger through Buffett's gift, the Bill & Melinda Gates Foundation is a traditional foundation, doing business in a longstanding way, one that would have been recognizable by Carnegie and Rockefeller, making grants to existing public charities and nonprofit organizations. The Gateses appropriated traditional concepts of education and public health to structure their foundation. They came to realize that the broader social, economic, and political issues of development must be tackled to achieve their desired global health goals and reduce inequities around the world.

The foundation's size allows it to do things beyond the reach of nearly all other foundations. Its resources, in terms of its endowment, its investment income, Buffett's annual gifts, and its grants, makes its potential for aid to the Third World larger than all but several existing nations.

Yet other donors have only slowly embraced the projects funded by the Gates Foundation. Their slowness may stem from their financial constraints, ambivalence (if not suspicion) about particular projects, alternative causes, such as global warming, or a belief that the Gates Foundation by itself provides sufficient support for a project. For example, in 2005, support for new research into vaccines and drugs to treat tuberculosis remained nearly stagnant, with public sector contributions dropping and the most of the shortfall made good by the Gates Foundation.[56]

It brings a pragmatic, businesslike approach to twenty-first century philanthropy. Seven points are of importance. First, it is deep into strategic vision. The Gateses are heavily hands on and involved in formulating and refining its strategies.

Second, it hopes to achieve a measurable impact through targeted grants in its three specific programmatic areas. The foundation has a clear, but limited focus.

Third, it actively seeks out organizations to receive funding in these three areas. It does not passively process donation requests and then dole out the money.

Fourth, by specializing and focusing on a few, well-chosen areas and sticking to them, its expertise helps it take calculated risks. It typically gains input from outsiders, relying on committees of outside experts not only with respect to its program and strategy development but also for guidance on whom to fund and how much to award in its grant-making.

In taking on some of the largest challenges known to humanity, it places big "bets" on grantees it thinks will be effective. Realizing that risk and reward are linked, it is influential because it is not afraid to fail and thus can support long-shot projects with perhaps a minimal chance of success. As a risk-taking foundation rather than a governmental entity or a business organization, it can handle the risks of one hundred million dollar failures. However, it faces significant scientific challenges in meeting some of its health goals. Even if its new products gain regulatory approval, it faces the need to reach those who need them, including the very poor living in inaccessible rural areas. The challenges of delivering new products may be beyond the capacity of the foundation.

Fifth, in its grant-making, it has made prolific use of partnerships. It has provided incentives to pharmaceutical companies to develop drugs for poor people in the Third World that they otherwise would not have considered doing. It has worked with governments, international agencies, and other foundations. As Bill Gates indicated, "But no foundation alone can solve the health problems of the developing world. We need businesses and governments as partners. That means we need to get these issues on the political agenda, and we need to tap into market forces to get the private sector involved. It means we all need to embrace a broader definition of responsibility."[57]

The Gates Foundation has led the way in making philanthropists realize that to make a difference they must often find strategic partners. In implementing this approach, for example, the Gates Foundation entered into a partnership in September 2006 with the Rockefeller Foundation to establish the Alliance for a Green Revolution in Africa to raise agricultural productivity in Africa by increasing access to seeds for local crops that will produce higher yields. While focusing on developing new varieties of seeds for primary foodstuffs, the effort will also entail university level training for African crop scientists and restructuring seed distribution systems, using small entrepreneurs in rural areas.[58]

Sixth, in addition to doing research, primarily outsourced to outside experts, who know where its grants can have the most likely impact, it sets clear expectations about how it expects its grantees to spend its funds. Gates' grants generally provide specific deliverables, target dates, and benchmarks for success.

Seventh, it uses performance management techniques to assess its grantees' success. Although working with grantees to help them achieve their aims, it applies a rigorous approach to evaluating the outcome of its grants, whether or not positive, generally outsourcing the evaluation process and candidly disclosing its failures, such as its inability to make measurable progress in high school math achievement rates.[59] In response to critics who point to a lack of transparency, it now provides more information on its website, including case studies of its grantees to describe what is working and what has not worked. By evaluating its grants to monitor their effectiveness and measure their impact and stopping funding when failure (or even long-term success) results, the Gates Foundation demonstrates how it is a source of discipline for its grantees.

In striving to create a way to measure results, through performance-based rigor and accountability, it faces a dilemma: it is difficult to measure a grant's impact. More generally, it is unclear what standards ought to be used to measure philanthropic returns. Furthermore, some of the social problems it seeks to solve, such as American students dropping out of high school or even graduating without mastering essential skills, may be so complex and intractable as to be insoluble without significant restrictions, such as limiting the choices people make about their lives, that may be impossible to impose and would, in any event, not be tolerated in a democratic society.

Is the Private Foundation Model Outmoded?

In identifying specific problems and designing a strategy often calling for a mix of scientific research and money to find solutions, the Gates Foundation runs into federal restrictions on its activities. In 1969, Congress responded to complaints that private foundations, such as Carnegie and Rockefeller, were elitist and may have played too large a role in our democracy. To ensure that foundations use their resources for charitable purposes, detailed operating restrictions and accompanying excise taxes are imposed on private foundations to compensate for their lack of public accountability.

Today, to curb what Congress perceived as abusive behavior, private foundations are subject to six excise taxes designed to restrict their activities.

Self-Dealing. Private foundations are subject to self-dealing rules. The Internal Revenue Code imposes an excise tax on any "disqualified person" who engages in an act of self-dealing with a private foundation as well as on any foundation manager who participates in an act of self-dealing.[60] Disqualified persons include the foundation's managers, substantial contributors to the foundation, and any person who owns more than 20 percent of an entity that is a substantial contributor to the foundation.[61] Self-dealing acts include, among others, any sale or exchange of property between a foundation and the disqualified person, the lending of money, or the furnishing of goods or services.

Distributions. Private foundations must make minimum annual distributions from their investment income to accomplish their charitable purposes. The Internal Revenue Code directs foundations to make "qualifying distributions" each year of at least 5 percent of basically the fair market value of their net investment assets.[62] A number of restrictions, beyond the scope of this book, exist as to the types of grants that may be used to satisfy the minimum distribution requirement. Any additional, undistributed income is subject to an excise tax.

Excess Business Holdings. An excise tax is imposed on a private foundation's "excess business holdings."[63] Excess business holdings are defined as ownership interests in a business in excess of 20 percent (or in some cases 35 percent) held by the foundation, its managers, or its substantial contributors in a business enterprise.

Jeopardy Investments. Any private foundation and its managers that make an investment jeopardizing the carrying out of the foundation's exempt purposes is subject to an excise tax.[64] Treasury Regulations provide that a jeopardizing investment is one for which a foundation manager "failed to exercise ordinary business care and prudence, under the facts and circumstances prevailing at the time of making the investment, in providing for the long- and short-term financial needs of the foundation in carrying out its exempt purposes."[65]

Although exceptions exist to the jeopardizing investment excise tax rules, the penalties for making "jeopardizing investments" can be severe. The first tier tax equals 10 percent of the amount of the jeopardizing investment when it was made. This 10 percent tax is imposed on both the foundation and any foundation manager (subject to a $10,000 maximum for the latter) who knowingly participated in making the investment. If the IRS does not abate this first tier tax and if the jeopardizing investment is not corrected within a "reasonable" time, the IRS may impose a second tier tax equal to 25 percent of the amount of the jeopardizing investment on the foundation and 5 percent on the foundation manager (subject to a $20,000 maximum for the latter).

An exception to the jeopardizing investment excise tax rules exists for program-related investments.[66] A program-related investment (PRI) is an investment having three characteristics. First, its primary purpose is to accomplish one or more of the foundation's exempt purposes, that is, the investment significantly furthers the foundation's tax-exempt activities. Second, no significant purpose of the investment is to produce income or capital appreciation. If the terms of the investment are less favorable than for-profit investors would require given the same risks, the production of income test will likely be met. Third, no purpose of the investment is to influence legislation or take part in political campaigns on behalf of candidates.[67] The last test is met if the recipient of the investment represents that none of the funds will be used to influence legislation or any political campaign.

Program-related investments typically take the form of low-interest loans that foundations provide to nonprofits. These loans help nonprofits establish a credit and repayment history often helping them get future bank financing. Because PRIs partially demonstrate sustainability to commercial investors they also facilitate financial discipline.

For example, in 2007, in addition to a $5.4 million grant, the Gates Foundation made a $10 million program-related investment in Opportunity International USA, a nonprofit, faith-based, global provider of microfinance services through its network of local implementing partners. As one of the leaders in the microfinance field, Opportunity International, through grants, loans, and equity investments in its implementing partners, makes microcredit loans to over 900,000 people annually in twenty-eight countries. The Gates PRI took the form of a loan, to be repaid over ten years at 1 percent interest, which will be used to help fund microfinance banks in Rwanda, Uganda, Kenya, and the Democratic Republic of the Congo, during their second and third years of operation. This is typically a difficult time for a MFO to attract sufficient savings deposits and/or commercial debt needed to generate growth. The PRI loan also will help the MFOs meet minimum capital requirements set by regulatory authorities and provide funds for more loans to poor clients.[68]

Foundations can make program-related investments in various organizations, including some for-profit entities. In January 2007 the Gates Foundation made a combined $9 million grant and a $20 million PRI in the form of a subordinated loan to ProCredit Holding, a for-profit entity discussed in Chapter 4. These funds will enable ProCredit to expand its banking operations in Africa.[69]

Foundations generally, however, are leery of extending program-related investments to for-profit businesses because they can be risky. For example, many of the 15 percent of program-related investments that the Ford Foundation has written off over the years went to for-profit businesses run by nonprofits rather than for the operations of nonprofits.[70]

To ensure that program-related investments further a foundation's exempt purpose, it must exercise "expenditure responsibility,"[71] next discussed.

Taxable Expenditures. The Internal Revenue Code imposes an excise tax on "taxable expenditures."[72] Generally speaking, taxable expenditures include amounts paid or incurred to: 1) attempt to influence legislation, such as lobbying; 2) influence the outcome of any specific public election; or 3) payments to persons or entities (with certain exceptions). Thus, grants to organizations, including program-related investments, are taxable expenditures, unless the recipients are certain public entities or the foundation exercises "expenditure responsibility" with respect to the grant. In brief, expenditure responsibility entails monitoring and documenting a grant or a program-related investment. Documentation includes financial recordkeeping and reporting as well as a written commitment by the recipient organization to use the funds for specified purposes and not to influence legislation or elections.

Finally, private foundations also are required to submit detailed information on their annual exempt organization returns, IRS Form 999-PF.[73] These returns are publicly available and must include reports on grants and program-related investments as to which the foundation has expenditure responsibility.

Although a traditional foundation, the Bill & Melinda Gates Foundation is unique in its sheer size, which allows it to do what other foundations cannot. Nevertheless, it represents an old-guard methodology that others are rebelling against, rather than an ideal to be emulated. However, few would argue with the impact the Gates Foundation has had, and will continue to have, on the world. The only question is whether the new style of philanthropy can be even more effective in achieving various goals.

In addition to seeking to avoid the restrictions imposed on private foundations, other donors seek to blur the lines between philanthropy and business. In striving to do good and generate profits, they view the traditional foundation model, built on the fortunes of earlier industrial giants, such as Carnegie and Rockefeller, and now followed by Gates, as too hidebound and often ineffective for their purposes.

Notes

1. Julie Bick, "The Microsoft Millionaires Come of Age," *New York Times*, May 29, 2005, Section 3, 5.
2. For comparisons between Carnegie-Rockefeller and Gates, I have drawn on Daniel Gross, "Giving It Away, Then and Now," *New York Times*, July 2, 2006, Section 3, 4.

3. Numerous books trace Gates and the Microsoft empire, including Bill Gates with Nathan Myhrvold and Peter Rinearson, *The Road Ahead*, revised edition (New York: Penguin, 1996); James Wallace and Jim Erickson, *Hard Drive: Bill Gates and the Making of the Microsoft Empire*, (New York: HarperBusiness, 1992); Stephen Mannes and Paul Andrews, *Gates: How Microsoft's Mogul Reinvented an Industry and Made Himself the Richest Man in America*, (New York: Doubleday, 1993); Jennifer Edstrom and Marlin Eller, *Barbarians Led By Bill Gates: Microsoft From The Inside* (New York: Henry Holt, 1998). *See also*, Brent Schlender and Henry Goldblatt, "Bill & Paul Talk," *Fortune* 132:7 (October 2, 1995): 68-86; Brent Schlender and Kate Ballen, "What Bill Gates REALLY Wants," *Fortune* 131:1 (January 16, 1995): 34-63; John Seabrook, "E-mail from Bill," *New Yorker* 69:45 (January 10, 1994): 48-61; Alan Deutschman and Mark D. Fefer, "Bill Gates' Next Challenge," *Fortune* 126:14 (December 28, 1992); 30-41; Richard Brandt, "The Billion-Dollar Whiz Kid," *BusinessWeek* 2993 (April 13, 1987): 68-76.
4. Peter Newcome and Harold Sencke, "The Forbes 400," *Forbes* 156:9 (October 16, 1995): 108-273, at 108-109.
5. Matthew Miller and Tatiana Serafin, "The Forbes 400," *Forbes* 178:7 (October 9, 2006): 80-184, at 81.
6. Luisa Knoll with Matthew Miller, "Billionaire Rankings," *Forbes* 181:6 (March 24, 2008), 146-160, at 150 and Luisa Kroll and Allison Fass, "The World's Billionaires," *Forbes* 179:6 (March 26, 2007): 104-184, at 105, 154.
7. Bill Gates, "Gates Harvard Commencement Speech," June 7, 2007 <http://online.wsj.com/article_print.html>.
8. Michael Specter, "What Money Can Buy," *New Yorker* 81:33 (October 24, 2005): 57-71, at 65.
9. Andrew Jack, "The Casual-Trousered Philanthropists," *Financial Times* (London) *Weekend Magazine*, March 11, 2006, 14.
10. Bill & Melinda Gates Foundation, Announcement, "Bill and Melinda Gates Establish Library Foundation Dedicated to Bringing Internet to Libraries," June 23, 1997 <http://www.gatesfoundation.org/United States/USLibraryProgram/Announcements/Announce-81.htm> (September 18, 2007). See also Warren Wilson, "Gateses Open Book on Library Venture," *Seattle Post-Intelligencer*, June 23, 1997, B1; Steve Lohr, "Gates to Help Libraries Acquire Gear to Go on Line," *New York Times*, June 24, 1997, D1.
11. Bill & Melinda Gates Foundation, 2005 Annual Report, 17.
12. Bill & Melinda Gates Foundation, Press Release, "Gates Foundation Confirms Increase in Endowment as reported in Newsweek," August 22, 1999. See also, Neil Modie, "Gateses Now Claim Largest Charity," *Seattle Post-Intelligencer*, August 23, 1999, A1; Doug Levy, "Gates Pours $6B More into Foundation," *USA Today*, August 23, 1999, 1B.
13. Bill & Melinda Gates Foundation, "Our Values" <http://www.gatesfoundation.org/AboutUS/OurValues> (April 9, 2007). Useful overviews of the Bill & Melinda Gates Foundation include Jean Strouse, "How to Give Away $21.8 Billion," *New York Times Magazine* (April 16, 2000), 56-63, 78, 88, 96, 101; Karl Taro Greenfeld, "Giving Billions Isn't Easy," *Time* 154:4 (July 24, 2000): 52-53; Jolayne Houtz, "Gates Foundation Wields New-Found Clout," *Seattle Times*, October 28, 2001, A1; Sebastian Mallaby, "Opening the Gates," *Washington Post*, April 5, 2004, A17; Amanda Ripley and Amanda Bower, "From Riches to Rags," *Time* 166:26 (December 26, 2005): 72-88; Specter, "What Money Can Buy," 65-66, 71.
14. Bill Gates, "The Way We Give," *Fortune* 155:1 (January 22, 2007): 41-46, at 42.

15. United States v. Microsoft Corp., Complaint, U.S. District Court for The District of Columbia, May 18, 1998.
16. United States v. Microsoft Corp., 84 F. Supp. 2d 9(DDC 1999) (findings of fact that Microsoft Corp. enjoyed monopoly power in the marketing of the licensing of operating systems for personal computers); United States v. Microsoft Corp., 87 F. Supp. 2d 30(DDC 1999) (conclusions of law that Microsoft maintained its monopoly power in the operating system market by anticompetitive means); United States v. Microsoft Corp., 253 F. 3d 34 (DC Cir. 2001).
17. United States v. Microsoft Corp., Stipulation and Revised Proposed Final Judgment, Civil Action No. 98-1232(CKK), U.S. District Court for the District of Columbia, November 2001. See also Stephen Labaton with Steve Lohr, "U.S. and Microsoft in Deal, but States Hold Back," *New York Times*, November 3, 2001, A1.
18. Internal Revenue Code (I.R.C.) §170.
19. I.R.C. § 2516.
20. Washington Revised Code §11.110.120.
21. Advisory Committee on Tax Exempt and Government Entities, "Report of Recommendations," June 13, 2007, 4.
22. Bill & Melinda Gates Foundation, Internal Revenue Service, 2005 990-PF, Part II.
23. Letter, Warren E. Buffett to Mr. And Mrs. William H. Gates III, June 26, 2006; Carol J. Loomis, "A Conversation with Warren Buffet," June 25, 2006 <*http://money.cnn.com/2006/06/25/ magazines/fortune/charitiy2.fortune/index.htm*> (April 16, 2007); Carol J. Loomis, "Warren Buffett Gives It Away," *Fortune* 154:1 (July 10, 2006): 56-69. See also *Economist*, "The New Powers in Giving" 380:8484 (July 1, 2006): 63-65; Andrew Jack, "How Buffett Gave a Call to Alms," *Financial Times* (London), June 28, 2006, 14; Donald G. McNeil Jr. and Rick Lyman, "Buffett's Billions Will Aid Fight Against Disease," *New York Times*, June 27, 2006, A1; Brooke A. Masters and Yugi Noguchi, "Corporate Titans Create a Colossal Charity," *Washington Post*, June 27, 2006, A1; Sally Beatty, Marilyn Chase, Gautum Naik, "How $60 Billion Behemoth Will Affect World of Charity," *Wall Street Journal*, June 27, 2006, B1. The longstanding friendship between Warren Buffett and Bill Gates is detailed in Landon Thomas Jr., "A Gift between Friends," *New York Times*, June 27, 2006, C1. Stephanie Strom examines the pressure on foundations to make funds flow out faster in "How Long Should Gifts Just Grow?," *New York Times*, November 12, 2007, H1.
24. Andrew Jack, "How Buffett Gave a Call to Alms."
25. For a critique of the Gates Foundation's holdings in many corporations that failed various tests of social responsibility and ethical conduct see Charles Piller, Edmund Sanders, and Robyn Dixon, "Dark Cloud over Good Works of Gates Foundation," *Los Angeles Times*, January 7, 2007, A1; Charles Piller, "Money Clashes with Mission," *Los Angeles Times*, January 8, 2007, A1. For the foundation's response see Bill & Melinda Gates Foundation, "Our Investment Philosophy" <*http://www.gatesfoundation.org/AboutUs/OurWork/Financials*> (February 12, 2008) and Patty Stonesifer, "A Foundation States Its Case," *Los Angeles Times*, January 14, 2007, M5. See also Charles Piller, "Gates Foundation to Keep Its Investment Approach," *Los Angeles Times*, January 14, 2007, A23; Charles Piller, "Gates Foundation to Weigh New Limits," *Los Angeles Times*, January 12, 2007, C3; Andrew Jack, "Keeping up with the Gateses," *Financial Times* (London), December 11, 2007, FT Report - Understanding Global Philanthropy 2007, 5; *Investor's Business Daily*, "Bill Gates Owes No Apologies," January 16, 2007, A19.

26. Declaration of Trust for The Bill & Melinda Gates Foundation, as of January 4, 2005.
27. Bill & Melinda Gates Foundation, "Making Progress in Our Century," November 29, 2006 <http://www.gatesfoundation.org/AboutUs/Announcements/Announce-061129.htm> (April 18, 2007) and Bill & Melinda Gates Foundation, "About the Bill & Melinda Gates Foundation Asset Trust," May 31, 2007 <http:www.gatesfoundation.org/AboutUs/Announcements> (February 12, 2008). See also Ian Wilhelm, "Gates Foundation Announces That It Doesn't Plan to Operate Forever," *Chronicle of Philanthropy* 19:5 (December 7, 2006): 7.
28. Bill & Melinda Gates Foundation, "Letter from Bill and Melinda Gates" <http://www.gatesfoundation.org/AboutUs/OurValues/GatesLetter.htm> (April 9, 2007).
29. Bill Gates, "The Way We Give," 42.
30. "Gates Harvard Commencement Speech." See also Robert A. Guth, "The Speechmaker," *Wall Street Journal*, June 8, 2007, A1.
31. Bill & Melinda Gates Foundation, 2006 Annual Report, 21, 25, 26; Bill & Melinda Gates Foundation, 2005 Annual Report, 5-9. See also Tamar Lewin, "Young Students Become the New Cause for Big Donors," *New York Times*, August 21, 2005, Section 1, 21.
32. Bill & Melinda Gates Foundation, 2006 Annual Report, 24.
33. I have drawn on Bill & Melinda Gates Foundation, "The Face of Change," 2005 Annual Report, 11-16. See also Erika Check, "Quest for the Cure," *Foreign Policy* 155 (July 1, 2006): 28:26, 34-35.
34. Specter, "What Money Can Buy," *New Yorker*, 65-66. See also "Gates Harvard Commencement Speech."
35. Gates, "The Way We Give," 44, 46. See also Bill & Melinda Gates Foundation, "Our Guiding Principles" <http://www.gatesfoundation.org/AboutUs/OurValues/GuidingPrinciples> (April 9, 2007).
36. See generally Dr. Richard Klausner, "Global Health: The 21st Century Challenge of Science, Technology and Society," January 4, 2005 <http://www.gatesfoudation.org/MediaCenter/Speeches/GHSpeeches> (September 16, 2007). The Gates Foundation's efforts to combat malaria in Africa are chronicled in Sandi Doughton, "Gates Foundation Tackle a Giant That Preys on Africa's Children," *Seattle Times*, September 23, 2007, A1; Sandi Doughton, "Disease Fighters Cast Their Net for Simpler, Basic Protections," *Seattle Times*, September 24, 2007, A1; Kristi Heim, "Salesmanship Joins Science in Struggle against Disease," *Seattle Times*, September 25, 2007, A1. For a critique of the foundation's healthcare efforts see Charles Piller and Doug Smith, "Unintended Victims," *Los Angeles Times*, December 16, 2007, A1 and Donald G. McNeil Jr., "W.H.O. Official Complains of Gates Foundation Dominance in Malaria Research," *New York Times*, February 16, 2008, A6. See also *Economist*, "The Side-Effects of Doing Good," 386:8568 (February 23, 2008): 77-78; and Sandi Doughton, "Not Many Speak Their Mind to World's Biggest Donor," *Seattle Times*, August 3, 2008, A1.
37. Bill & Melinda Gates Foundation, Press Release, "Fourteen Grand Challenges in Global Health Announced in $200 Million Initiative, October 16, 2003 and Bill & Melinda Gates Foundation, 2005 Annual Report, 13. See also Donald G. McNeil Jr., "New Ideas in Global Health Get a $437 Million Assist," *New York Times*, June 28, 2005, F1; Elizabeth Corcoran, "Chutzpah Science," *Forbes* 176:2 (July 25, 2005): 64; Tom Paulson, "A Challenge to Scientists," *Seattle Post-Intelligencer*, October 17, 2003, A1.
38. Bill & Melinda Gates Foundation, Press Release, "New Grants Initiative to Spur Innovative Research in Global Health," October 9, 2007.

39. Ripley and Bower, "From Riches to Rags," 77.
40. Bill & Melinda Gates Foundation, Press Release, "Bill & Melinda Gates Foundation Announces $750 Million Gift to Speed Delivery of Life-Saving Vaccines," November 23, 1999; Bill & Melinda Gates Foundation, Press Release, "Gates Foundation, Norway Contribute $1 Billion to Increase Child Immunization in Developing Countries," January 24, 2005; Bill & Melinda Gates Foundation, "The Response" *<http:www.gatesfoundation.org/AboutUs/OurWork/Learning/GAVI>* (September 16, 2007). See also Rachel Zimmerman, "A Shot in the Arm," *Wall Street Journal*, December 3, 2001, A1.
41. Statement by Bill Gate on the Launch of the International Finance Facility for Immunization, September 9, 2005 *<http://www.gatesfoundation.org/GlobalHealth/Pri_Diseases/Vaccines>* (September 16, 2007) and Bill & Melinda Gates Foundation, 2005 Annual Report, 15. See also Celia W. Dugger, "Billions for Vaccines for the Poor to Be Raised in Bond Markets," *New York Times*, September 9, 2005, A10; Joanna Chung, "New Bond Raises Dollars 1bn for Child Jabs," *Financial Times* (London), November 8, 2006, 45; Ben Hall and Andrew Gack, "Novel UK Funding for Vaccines Is Approved," *Financial Times* (London), August 3, 2005, 8.
42. Bill & Melinda Gates Foundation, Press Release, "Foundation Announces New Organization, New Presidents," April 12, 2006; Bill & Melinda Gates Foundation, "Financial Services for the Poor Backgrounder" *<http://www.gatesfoundation.org/GlobalDevelopment/FinancialServices>* (September 20, 2007) and "Agricultural Development Backgrounder" *<http://www.gatesfoundation.org/GlobalDevelopment/Agriculture/Ag>* (September 20, 2007); Bill & Melinda Gates Foundation, Press Release, "$306 Million Commitment to Agricultural Development," January 25, 2008. See also Ian Wilhelm, "Gates Foundation to Support New Causes," *Chronicle of Philanthropy* 18:13 (April 20, 2006): 10; Robert A. Guth, "Gates Expands Farm Grants," *Wall Street Journal*, January 25, 2008, B6; Kristi Heim, "Gates Pours Aid into African Coffee Farms," *Seattle Times*, January 25, 2008, A25; Kristi Heim, "Agricultural Aid a Hard Sell," *Seattle Times*, January 20, 2008, B1.
43. For background I have drawn on Connie Bruck, "Millions for Millions," *New Yorker* 82: 35 (October 30, 2006): 62-73; Ben Gose, "The Big Promise of Small Loans," *Chronicle of Philanthropy* 18:19 (July 20, 2006): 18-20 and James C. Brau and Gary M. Woller, "Microfinance: A Comprehensive Review of the Existing Literature," *Journal of Entrepreneurial Finance & Business Ventures* 9:1 (April 2004): 1-26.
44. Anita Hawser, "Big Banks Eye Micro Market," *Global Finance Magazine* 21:6 (June 2007): 24-26.
45. Claire Cain Miller, "Easy Money," *Forbes* 178:11 (November 27, 2006): 134-138, at 138.
46. David Hulme and Karen Moore, "Why Has Microfinance Been a Policy Success in Bangladesh (And Beyond)?," Global Policy Research Group-WPS-041, 10 March 2006; Robert Eichfeld and Henry Wendt, "Building on Success," *American Enterprise Institute Development Policy Outlook*, Number 4, 2006; Nathanael Goldberg, "Measuring the Impact of Microfinance: Taking Stock of What We Know," *Grameen Foundation USA Publication Series*, December 2005.
47. T. Dichter, "Hype and Hope: The Worrisome State of the Microcredit Movement," Consultative Group to Assist the Poor, 2006 *<http://www.micrifinancegateway.org/content/article/detail/3174>* (July 8, 2007).

48. MicroVest, "About Microfinance-Myths-Viability/Profitability of Microfinance Institutions <*MicroVest/About/Microfinance/Myths.htm*> (January 7, 2007). See also Paul J. Davies, "Industry set to grow 10-fold," *Financial Times* (London), November 16, 2007, 18.
49. Bruck, "Millions for Millions," 65.
50. *Ibid.*, 72.
51. bid., 68.
52. I have drawn on Pro Mujer, "Mission" <*http://www.promujer.org/mission.html*> (April 9, 2007); Pro Mujer, "Country programs" <*http://www.promujer.org/index*> (April 9, 2007); Pro Mujer, "Credit and Training Services" <*http://www.promujer.org/credits.html*> (April 9, 2007); Pro Mujer International, 2005 Annual Report, 3. See also Mercedes Olivera, "Program to Help Women in Mexico Spreads South," *Dallas Morning News*, June 23, 2007, 9B and Marla Dickinson, "They Pave Their Own Way With a Little Help," *Los Angeles Times*, September 10, 2006, C1.
53. Pro Mujer International, Press Release, "Gates Foundation Awards Pro Mujer $3.1 Million to Develop Innovative Microcredit Products," April 26, 2006. See also Rosemary Werrett, "The Future of Microfinance," *Worth* 15:11 (November 2006): 32.
54. Unitus, "Frequently Asked Questions: General Questions About Unitus" <*http://www.unitus.com/sections/aboutus_faq_main.asp*> (April 13, 2007) and "Our Strategy" <*http://www.unitus.com/sections/aboutus/aboutus_os.asp*> (December 20, 2006). See also TheMIXMarket, "Profile for Unitus" <*http://www.mixmarket.org/en*> (April 13, 2007); Tricia Duryee, "Microfinance gets VC nudge," *Seattle Times*, May 22, 2006, E1.
55. Unitus, Inc., Press Release, "Unitus and Bill & Melinda Gates Foundation Launch Microfinance Efficiency Initiative," October 26, 2006. See also, Kristi Heim, "Gates Grant to Aid Unitus in Improving Microfinance," *Seattle Times*, October 20, 2006, D1; Jay Greene, "Taking Tiny Loans to the Next Level," *BusinessWeek* 4011 (November 27, 2006): 76. The donation from Gates followed a $2.7 million grant from The Omidyar Network in September 2005 to enable Unitus to expand its operations and hire key staff members. Unitus, Press Release, "Unitus Announces $2.7 Million Grant from Omidyar Network," September 30, 2005.
56. Jack, "Keeping up" and Cindra Fever, *Tuberculosis Research and Development: A Critical Analysis of Funding Trends, 2005-2006* (New York: Treatment Action Group, 2007), 20-22.
57. Gates, "The Way We Give," 46.
58. Bill & Melinda Gate Foundation, Press Release, "Bill & Melinda Gates, Rockefeller Foundations Form Alliance to Help Spur 'Green Revolution' in Africa," September 12, 2006 and Bill & Melinda Gates Foundation, 2006 Annual Report, 11. See also Stephanie Strom, "2 Foundations Join in Africa Agriculture Push," *New York Times*, September 13, 2006, A16; Karen DeYoung "Gates, Rockefeller Charities Join to Fight African Hunger," *Washington Post*, September 13, 2006, A1.
59. Bill & Melinda Gates Foundation, The National Evaluation of High School Transformation, "Getting to Results: Students Outcomes in New and Redesigned High Schools," July 2005, 4. See also Bill & Melinda Gates Foundation, 2005 Annual Report, 9 and David Herszenhorn, "In New York's Smaller Schools, 'Good Year and a Tough Year'," *New York Times*, August 8, 2005, A1. But see Bill & Melinda Gates Foundation, Announcements, "New Study Says NYC Small High School Reforms Boost Student Performance," January 30, 2007; Julie Bosman, "New

Small Schools Show Higher Graduation Rates," *New York Times*, June 30, 2007, A15. For evaluations of the Gates Foundation high school grants, see American Institute For Research, *Executive Summary: Evaluation of the Bill & Melinda Gates Foundation's High School Grants, 2001-2004*, n.d.; American Institutes for Research, *Creating Cultures for Learning: Supportive Relationships in New and Redesigned High Schools*, April 2005; American Institutes for Research, *Getting to Results: Students Outcomes in New and Redesigned High Schools, July 2005*; American Institutes for Research, *Rigor, Relevance, and Results: The Quality of Teacher Assignments and Student Work in New and Conventional High Schools*, July 2005.
60. I.R.C. §4941.
61. I.R.C. §4946(a).
62. I.R.C. §4942.
63. I.R.C. § 4943.
64. I.R.C. § 4944.
65. Treasury Regulations §53.4944-1(a)(2)(I).
66. I.R.C. §4944(c).
67. Treasury Regulations §53.4944-3(a)(1).
68. Opportunity International, Press Release, "Gates Foundation Provides $15.4 Million to Opportunity International to Help Build Microfinance Banks in Five African Nations," February 20, 2007. See also Bill & Melinda Gates Foundation, 2006 Annual Report, 12. In November 2005, the Gates Foundation donated $2.2 million to Opportunity International to develop a trans-African network of new commercial banks for the poor. Opportunity International, Press Release, "Opportunity International Receives $2.2 Million Grant from the Bill and Melinda Gates Foundation, November 30, 2005.
69. ProCredit Holding AG, Press Release, "Gates Foundation and ProCredit Holding forge a partnership to promote the expansion of commercial microfinance in Africa," January 23, 2007.
70. Stephanie Strom, "Make Money, Saving the World," *New York Times*, May 6, 2007, Section 3, 1.
71. I.R.C. §4945(h).
72. I.R.C. §4945.
73. I.R.C. §6033.

4

Pierre Omidyar and Omidyar Network: Pioneering Hybrid Philanthropy

Pierre Omidyar, the founder of eBay, is one of the world's richest people. In October 2007, *Forbes* placed his net worth at $8.9 billion, ranking him at number 32 among the richest people in America.[1] In March 2008, *Forbes* estimated his net worth at $7.7 billion, ranking him at number 120 among the globe's billionaires.[2] Omidyar's wealth came almost overnight during the mid- to late-1990s when the dot com market was surging. When the market crashed, only a few companies from this period had the staying power to survive, and Omidyar's eBay was one of them. He emerged from this period a billionaire.

Quite different from Gates, Omidyar has chosen to invest and distribute this wealth in unusual ways. He is at the forefront of blurring the lines between the for-profit and nonprofit worlds, pioneering in creating the structural shift known as hybrid philanthropy, striving to improve lives, regardless of the mechanism.

Omidyar's experience at eBay informed his approach to philanthropy. He has long been interested in the power of the Internet to connect people and in the natural entrepreneurial instinct of individuals. Through Omidyar Network, founded in 2005, he invests in for-profit and nonprofit initiatives designed to promote individual empowerment, economic, social or political, enabling people to tap their potential to make a difference. Omidyar sees these opportunities to help people discover their own power in both the business and social sectors.

Few efforts blur the line between doing good and making money as dramatically as the for-profit microfinance programs championed by Omidyar. In addition to blending philanthropy and for-profit business, he has focused on microfinance as a poverty alleviation strategy through economic empowerment. Muhammad Yunus, the founder of Grameen Bank in Bangladesh and the 2006 Nobel Peace Prize winner, pioneered the microcredit concept discussed in Chapter 3. Omidyar is now doing something Yunus is skeptical of: he believes that microfinance organizations can lift people out of poverty and as multi-faceted social impact entities some of which may generate profits at the same time.

Background on Pierre Omidyar

Pierre M. Omidyar[3] was born in France in 1967. He moved frequently as a child with his Iranian-French parents, learning that most things begin with community. He immigrated at age six with his parents to the Washington, DC area where his interest in computers bloomed. By seventh grade he had already taught himself how to program a computer.

Omidyar went to Tufts University in the mid-1980s to pursue his interest in computer programming. Tufts had a significant impact on how Omidyar came to view the Internet's dramatic potential. Included in the university's profile statement are three values to which it is committed: citizenship, that is, fostering an attitude of "giving back"; diversity; and a global orientation.[4] All of these became part of Omidyar's own vision of eBay's role in the global community as bringing people from diverse backgrounds together in an electronic marketplace.

While at Tufts, Omidyar taught himself how to program Apple computers, and by the time he was a junior, he realized that to fulfill his passion to become a Macintosh programmer he had to go to the West Coast. After receiving a B.S. in computer science in 1988, he joined Claris, a subsidiary of Apple Computer Inc., as a consumer software engineer in Silicon Valley. He then co-founded Ink Development Corp. in 1991 after Apple decided not to take Claris public. The startup company sought to create computers that operated using a hand-held stylus rather than a keyboard. This innovation would eventually catch on with PalmPilots, but in the early 1990s the market was not yet ready for it. The group at Ink spun off an online commerce project and relaunched itself as eShop. However, the venture was not moving toward the Internet fast enough for Omidyar. He wanted more contact with people and the Internet, and in 1994, he left eShop, two years before Microsoft Corp. bought the company. Omidyar had retained a significant ownership interest in eShop, and the stock he received from the buyout made him a millionaire at age twenty-nine.

While next working at General Magic, another Apple offshoot, he started a side project, which became eBay. In September 1995, he wrote a program enabling people to buy and sell items on the Internet. He realized the program's potential when he put a broken laser pointer up for sale on the new site, AuctionWeb. He advertised the pointer as busted and asked for $1; in two weeks, bids boosted the price and he sold the pointer for $14. The Internet auction concept was born.

In developing the program, he sought to create a perfect economic market where buyers and sellers would have equal access to information and an equal opportunity to use that information. He chose the auction format because, according to economic theory, an auction yields the perfect price. Items are sold where supply meets demand.

The site was a quick success. In March 1996, Omidyar's revenues hit $1,000 a month; by June, they reached $10,000. As the site grew, concerns surfaced over the reliability of sellers to follow through with delivery after transactions were consummated. Omidyar believed (and continues to believe) that people are usually good; therefore, Auction-Web relied primarily on an honor system. As a free market based on trust, hundreds of millions of users learned to trust strangers, a concept that revolutionized both commerce and the Internet. Yet Omidyar was not naïve. He also knew that some would try to take advantage of such trust, so he came up with the idea of the Feedback Forum in February 1996 as a tool to keep the system trustworthy. Registered users could give a buyer or seller a rating and write a comment. Positive and negative reviews about users would alert or pacify the fears of people doing business on the site. People became known by their reputation. If a rating was so poor, a person would be removed as a registered user.

In 1997 he changed the name of his firm to eBay, which was already the URL address for AuctionWeb, thus making the website easier to find. After eBay went public in September 1998, Omidyar's stock was worth about $4 billion.[5] He had become the globe's richest thirty-two-year-old.

Together with CEO Margaret (Meg) Whitman, Omidyar led eBay through Internet bubble and bust, and the firm came out on top. While other dot coms found themselves in the trash bin of cyberspace, eBay increased its revenues by an average 77 percent a year from 2000 to 2004.[6] eBay also expanded with its $1.5 billion acquisition of PayPal, an online payment service, in 2002. The firm then went beyond auctions, taking a stake in the online classified business, Craigslist, in 2004, and buying the comparison pricing site Shopping.com in 2005 and the web-telephone outfit Skype later that year.[7]

Omidyar's vision created a level playing field by connecting people with people through their shared interests. eBay continues to give ordinary people an economic foothold online. For Omidyar, eBay represents a prime example of economic empowerment. As of December 31, 2006, eBay had approximately 222 million registered users worldwide[8] thereby demonstrating the power of the Internet for Omidyar. ebay allowed people to change their lives; anyone could use it anywhere in the world. The eBay concept remains the single biggest influence on his philanthropic philosophy.

The Concept Behind eBay and Its Impact on Omidyar's Thinking

The eBay phenomenon represents Omidyar's philosophy on how markets should run. For Omidyar, a libertarian follower of Adam Smith's teachings, unrestrained market forces and self-interest produce the most efficient and socially beneficial use of capital. Yet the markets Omidyar often saw did not work this way in practice. Instead, he felt that a select group of favored individuals manipulated markets. This lesson was brought home to him in 1993 when he heard about a new video game company, 3DO, that was about to go public. He placed an order for shares, but when he checked his account he discovered that the stock had already risen 50 percent before his order had gone through. Favored buyers had been let in beforehand, leaving the rest of the public to fight for the scraps.

With eBay, however, everyone has access to the same information and everyone has an equal opportunity to do what they want with that information. eBay serves as the antithesis of what Omidyar saw were the everyday workings of financial markets where insiders became rich off of information denied to the public. Thus, eBay functions as a nearly perfect marketplace, which revolutionized commerce, although it must continue to deal with the challenge of buyers' skittishness about sellers they do not know through various strategies to reduce fraud.

Omidyar created eBay as a tool to empower small buyers and sellers. It represents a social impact, profit model based on empowering individuals who do not know each other. The trust of strangers inculcated on eBay, Omidyar believes, carried over to other online sites and even to real-life interactions. "People have learned that, in general, people are basically good. And we have demonstrated that [through eBay]." Besides trust, eBay had another powerful impact: "So that is an incredibly empowering thing when an individual discovers his or her own ability to generate economic value." In 2006, Omidyar estimated that 750,000 people (or more) made their living selling on eBay.[9] He recalled, "I could see regular people coming and saying, 'eBay changed my life because now I feel I contribute to the household's finances.' There was a sense of empowerment even in those early days, and it increasingly became clear to me that eBay has had a huge social impact in the process of running its core business, and it wasn't philanthropy."[10] He further indicated, "It's about giving someone the tools they need to make their own life successful, actually trusting them with something they might not have been allowed to touch before, which is money." He realized, "Business can be a force for good. You can make the world a better place *and* make money at the same time."[11] This belief arose out of the eBay concept, but it took Omidyar several years to discover that it could also be extended to philanthropy, namely, that business and benevolence were not divergent forces but instead could work together to become an enormous engine for positive change.

Establishment of The Omidyar Foundation

As Omidyar came to arrive at the conclusion that profit-making ventures could be a force for social good, similar to Gates, he first took a more traditional philanthropic route. After eBay went public in 1998, Omidyar found himself a multibillionaire. Pierre, together with his wife, Pamela, started The Omidyar Foundation in 1998 to give away large sums of money to nonprofits.

After several years, Pierre became frustrated by the constraints and inefficiencies of the nonprofit world, including the lack of a good feedback mechanism, such as a for-profit entity's bottom line. He became dissatisfied with the limitations of investing in nonprofits. Too many were less effective than they could be because of duplicative efforts and their failure to measure results. He also concluded that a foundation as the form for his philanthropy was too restrictive to serve his purposes.[12]

As a result, in 2004 Pierre and Pamela reorganized their philanthropy, creating a new umbrella organization, Omidyar Network (Network). The Omidyars designed the Network to invest in both nonprofit groups and for-profit companies that provide social benefits, thereby poking at the longstanding firewall between the nonprofit and the for-profit world. As Pierre recalled, "I don't see why we ought to make an artificial distinction that says for-profit is all about making money and only nonprofit is about helping people."[13]

Omidyar Network

Omidyar Network,[14] founded in 2004, has created a diverse portfolio designed to foster opportunity for people globally, across economic, political, and social realms, with investments in for-profit entities and grants to nonprofit ventures in a variety of fields, including microfinance as well as participatory media and online groups, which give people the tools to express their thoughts. According to Omidyar, "We feel a sense of responsibility and opportunity to put wealth to good use. We organized the Omidyar Network to invest not only in nonprofits but also in for-profits. We think of it like a $400 million venture fund to deploy over the next five years. It focuses on a very broad mission of encouraging self-empowerment.... We're interested in businesses and nonprofits that help connect people to information."[15]

Omidyar sees the largest potential for hybrid philanthropy in the twenty-first century is in getting people thinking about business as having a positive impact and helping fund these types of entities. He stated, "Business can be a force for good, and you can earn profit for doing good. That view is really informed by my experience with eBay, and its social impact."[16] Omidyar does, however, not "believe that there is a for-profit answer to everything. But if for-profit capital can do more good than it does today, foundations can concentrate their resources where they are most needed. The largest impact we can have with this wealth will be testing a theory that business can be a tool for good."[17] Thus, the Network intends to catalyze a new type of business in which social impact drives profitability, where no separation exists between an entity's social and business missions.

Omidyar Network serves as a vehicle for making both for-profit investments and nonprofit grants. Actually, the Network has three checkbooks: first, the Omidyar Network Fund, Inc., a traditional private foundation, for funding nonprofit organizations; the second, a limited liability company (LLC), the Omidyar Network, LLC, for investing in profit-making businesses; and the third to pay for its overhead, the Omidyar Network Services, LLC, a subsidiary of Omidyar Network, LLC.

The Network's mission is to foster "opportunity for people around the world." It supports institutions and structures that foster opportunities for individuals to tap their potential, "enabling them to improve their lives and make powerful, lasting contributions to their communities."[18] Through the Network, by funding citizen-driven models, Omidyar wants to help people connect on a global scale to work on issues they care about.[19]

The Network not only provides a platform for investments, grants, and research but also for lobbying, political advertising, and public policy advocacy, thereby expanding its reach and impact far beyond that of the typical private foundation, such as the Gates Foundation.

From the outset, Omidyar put the Network's staff of cautious investors and nonprofit do-gooders in one office. Everyone is responsible for both nonprofit and for-profit deals, and applies a for-profit due diligence standard to nonprofits. Its team of due diligence specialists emphasizes equal access to information, giving power to ordinary people, fostering social capital through connections around shared interests, and a sense of ownership among the participants. The Network must see the social potential before making a grant to a nonprofit entity or an investment in a for-profit business.

Grants to Nonprofits. The Network's philanthropic funding focuses on grants to nonprofit organizations seeking to create a social impact, particularly Internet groups which enable people to take their ideas and give them worldwide launch. It strives to fund citizen-based solutions to social problems, designed to shift decision-making power away from experts, through on-line tools.

For example, the Network funds DonorsChoose, Inc., a nonprofit website, Donorschoose.org, which allows K-12 public school teachers to post requests for funding class projects, not otherwise funded by the public sector. Donors browse the requests by geography or keyword, choose their favorite, fund the project, and receive a response from the students and teachers they help. The organization received a $2 million contribution from the Omidyar Network.[20]

DonorsChoose functions a grassroots organization on both the receiving and the giving end of the funding. Because teachers typically request small amounts from under $100 to a few thousand dollars, donors need not be large foundations or even wealthy persons. Individuals easily fund projects, such as "Where Did All the Pencils Go?" for $60, and a "Geological Field Trip" for $2,000,[21] through the website. Thus, DonorsChoose is much like eBay itself, except that instead of selling goods, teachers sell ideas to prospective donors who then monitor their money's journey. Donors obtain not only a choice of projects to fund, but also the direct impact and the accountability previously available only to major philanthropists.

Other nonprofits the Network has funded include: Ashoka, which funds social entrepreneurs; The Center for Effective Philanthropy, which works to help foundations improve their performance; The GlobalGiving Foundation, which provides an online marketplace, similar to DonorsChoose, connecting funders with nonprofit, locally-run, social and economic projects throughout the world; KaBOOM!, which works with communities to design, build, and maintain their own playgrounds; Modest Needs Foundation, which channels small amounts of money to help struggling people hurt by unexpected expenses; Rare, which trains local conservationists around the world that it hopes to link online; and YouthNoise, a social network for young people interested in various social causes.[22]

Investments in For-Profit Entities. As of April 2008, the Omidyar Network had committed $96 million out of its $217 million pool for-profit-making entities.[23] The Network's for-profit arm seeks to invest in profit-making ventures that produce significant social benefits, or advance social goals, yet generate market-rate returns. The Network looks for for-profit entities with inseparable social and business missions.

One of the Network's investments in 2006 and 2007, Prosper Marketplace, Inc., a for-profit company, operates an online person-to-person website, Prosper.com, which facilitates loans ranging from $50 to $25,000.[24] Similar to eBay, Prosper allows individuals to post an amount of money they require for whatever reason, such as paying off credit cards or starting a new business, and the maximum interest rate they are willing to pay for a three-year loan. Prospective lenders, who select borrowers based on criteria commonly used by traditional lenders, such as credit scores and credit histories as well as geography, profession, hobby, or life event, among other factors, then bid on making an unsecured loan, thereby driving the interest rate down until it reaches its lowest point. Borrowers obtain access to capital at lower interest rates than they could through traditional sources; lenders receive higher returns than on bank deposits while helping others. Prosper takes the bids with the lowest rates, combines them into one loan, and then handles the on-going loan administration tasks in return for a one time, 1 to 3 percent fee to borrowers and a .5 percent annual fee to lenders. Borrowers can join (or create) self-defined groups with specific interests or characteristics that may make them more attractive to some lenders. Group borrowers, who segment themselves, generally qualify for lower interest rates because they are subject to peer pressure to repay loans.

If a borrower defaults on a loan, a lender (or a number of lenders pooled into a group) lose the funds they lent. Internet lending may appear a risky venture given the relative lack of oversight. Prosper docks a borrower's credit score in the event of a default and sends a collection agency after him or her. However, with a 1 percent default rate and only 3 percent of loans three months or more delinquent, borrowers appear to meet their obligations; the annual site-wide return for lenders, after taking defaults into account, averages about 7.5 percent.[25] In short, Prosper operates on a trust mechanism similar to the one that helped eBay become successful.

Other for-profit investments by the Network include: digg, a user-driven, social content website and news platform that enables individuals to prioritize the content available on the Internet; InnoCentive, Inc., a research collaborative that allows innovation-based companies (for example, pharmaceutical companies) to post web-based challenges to scientists around the world; Linden Lab, the creator and operator of an online world, Second Life, where participants can create a virtual identity; and Socialtext, Inc., which provides software that allows users to collaborate on group documents.[26]

Omidyar's Focus on Third World Economic Development Through the Commercialization of Microfinance Organizations

Apart from its other grants and investments, the Omidyar Network has focused considerable energy and a significant chunk of its capital in funding and helping microfinance organizations (MFOs) in an effort to expand access to capital for them to grow to scale. To date, the Network has invested over $40 million in nonprofit and for-profit microfinance ventures.

For Pierre Omidyar, microfinance possesses eBay-like properties. Both are based on trust; both allow people to discover that they can be entrepreneurs; both demonstrate free-market economic principles; both are businesses whose profitability is linked to social impact. In other words, for Omidyar microfinance is congruent with his eBay experience.

Omidyar sees himself as an agent of global change through the social impact of microfinance organizations, including commercial entities. At the September 2005 Clinton Global Initiative Conference, Omidyar stated: "[F]or us, it's not just about alleviating poverty. It's about economic self-empowerment."[27] According to Omidyar, "I believe microfinance has huge potential, not only to eliminate global poverty, which is remarkable, but also to help people achieve social, economic and political empowerment. But in order to have any real impact, microfinance companies need to sustain themselves and grow. And to do that they need to focus on profits, not only social outcomes.... The big difference between companies and traditional charities is that companies can grow in a self-financing and sustainable way, while charities cannot, as they need a continuous injection of capital to survive."[28]

To reach a sufficient scale and meet the needs of hundreds of millions of people who want to start or expand small businesses, Omidyar believes MFOs must have access to the private capital markets. To tap private capital, an organization must provide a competitive investment return. To offer competitive returns to investors, an entity must operate on a profitable basis and think of itself as a business. According to Omidyar, if the microfinance sector wants to reach global scale and fund up to five hundred million people, "... you cannot do it with philanthropy capital. There is not enough charity capital out there."[29]

In November 2004, leaders of the high-tech community including Omidyar and the co-founders of Google, Sergey Brin and Larry Page (discussed in Chapter 7), gathered at the San Francisco home of John Doerr, a venture capitalist principal in one of the marquee venture firms, Kleiner Perkins Caufield & Byers, for a weekend session with Muhammad Yunus, the founder and managing director of Grameen Bank, which gives millions of poor people access to credit from which they would otherwise be excluded. Yunus's statement that the poor are natural entrepreneurs, because their business activities represent a matter of survival, struck Omidyar. "By giving them the tools, you unleash the entrepreneurial instinct," Omidyar recalled,[30] realizing that microfinance could help reach hundreds of millions of people throughout the world by providing enhanced access to capital, not information.

As his thinking crystallized, Omidyar's idea of microfinance began to differ somewhat from Yunus's. Yunus remains firmly in the social mission camp. After receiving his Ph.D. from Vanderbilt University, Yunus began his professional career as a professor of economics at Chittagong University in Dhaka, Bangladesh. Disillusioned by academia, in the 1970s he decided to go into the field to try to discover what would help people lift themselves out of poverty. His experiments led him in 1983 to found the Grameen Bank, the most widely replicated microcredit model, that makes uncollaterized, small loans to those too poor to borrow from commercial banks.[31]

Yunus's involvement with microcredit organizations (MCOs) was philanthropic from the start, and he wants it to stay that way. Although advocating long-term financial sustainability for MCOs and MFOs, he focuses more on maximizing the social benefits, as exemplified by Pro Mujer, an MFO considered in Chapter 3. Yunus sees microcredit as primarily a charitable effort, and worries that lenders will lose sight of this if they emphasize the business side of it. According to Yunus, "Let them [MCOs and MFOs] make money—but why do you want to make money off the poor people?... [Y]ou come to help them. When they have enough flesh and blood in their bodies, go and suck them, no problem. But, until then, don't do that. Whatever money you are taking away, keep it with them instead, so that they can come out more quickly from poverty."[32]

Yunus thus wants the microfinance system to look to and continue to rely on donations and public sector subsidies rather than become interested in money-making first and helping the poor second. He asserts that running MCOs and MFOs as for-profit businesses will leave the poorest behind. Because larger loans to the upper tiers of the poor will likely generate more profits, he reasons that the destitute will be left by the wayside. As to future sources of capital, he looks to investors who seek a broader return beyond an immediate monetary gain. However, apart from foundations and philanthropically-inclined individuals, how many will invest because they believe in a cause?

This was the question Omidyar struggled with, and his answer turned him somewhat from Yunus's philanthropic viewpoint of microfinance to one that can be characterized as multi-faceted and socially responsible. Omidyar wants to build a sustainable, scalable microfinance sector, including profit-making entities. He strives to harness the power of private capital markets, thereby alleviating poverty through economic self-empowerment. The benefit of this approach for Omidyar centers on these organizations growing much faster, reaching more borrowers and savers, and achieving sustainability if commercialized as profit-oriented entities, able to tap private capital markets, rather than the donor market which cannot provide sufficient funds for microloans to reach hundreds of millions of microentrepreneurs. Furthermore, as MCOs and MFOs grow in size and become more efficient through, for example, the better use of information technology and improved recordkeeping, the resulting savings will fuel their profit potential and lead to, along with increased competition for clients, lower interest rates for borrowers, at least that is the expectation. Demonstrating good performance and creditworthiness will, in turn, make more capital available to an MCO or an MFO to lend to more clients. Once microfinance is "scaled," that is, expanded to its full potential "it's a self-sustaining profitable model, which opens the door to reaching a large number of people who need to be reached by this tool of access to capital," Omidyar noted. Microcredit and microfinance organizations could eventually secure funds in private capital markets and no longer rely on donor and public sector funding. Because nonprofit MCOs and MFOs find it difficult to obtain long-term streams of grants from donors, generating funds and responding to the separate needs of donors become costly endeavors. Reliance on donated and public sector funds also subjects entities to the whims of donors and governments. Thus, Omidyar concluded, "Rather than saying it's going to cost forty-five billion dollars a year, this year, next year, and forever, you can think of it as an initial investment—but there's a cap to how much you're ever going to put in. That's the difference between microfinance and the typical sort of government aid or charity, which is an ongoing thing."[33]

Omidyar worries that if donors, not investors, continue as capital providers to MCOs and MFOs, they could retard the emergence of microfinance and its investment class. Too much donated money flowing to MCOs and MFOs could distort the market and keep institutional and other investors from entering as capital suppliers. However, before banks and other investors will lend to MCOs and MFOs they must be financially sustainable and creditworthy. As noted in Chapter 3, because only a few hundred MCOs and MFOs are financially viable today, grants from foundations and nongovernmental organizations as well as public sector subsidies will continue to play an important role, particularly in getting MCOs and MFOs going.

Omidyar Network's Investments in and Grants To Nonprofits in the Microfinance Sector

The Network's for-profit investments in the microfinance sector focus on funding MCO and MFOs, through various microfinance intermediaries (MFIs), on which it expects to make a financial return. It has also given grants to nonprofit microfinance entities.

For-profit Microfinance Investments. MFIs have introduced microfinance to the world of capital markets. They bridge the gap between MCOs and MFOs in the field and international capital markets, enabling MCOs and MFOs to tap global financial markets through a variety of means, including commercial bank loans, commercial paper, debt or equity financing, and bundling (more technically, the securitization) of

MCO and MFO loans. If investors, such as Omidyar Network, earn returns through MFIs commensurate with the risks they bear, a large-scale poverty alleviation funding mechanism may exist.

One such MFI, BlueOrchard Finance S.A., a privately-owned Swiss microfinance investment adviser and manager, works with financial institutions as well as institutional and private investors to help them invest in loans issued by MFOs. Through its various investment funds, BlueOrchard seeks to provide investors with stable and competitive financial returns and deliver an effective social impact in developing nations by encouraging microentrepreneurship. It uses strict financial criteria, to which the MFOs it supports must adhere, including investigating how an organization controls its growth, enforcing requirements regarding overdue interest payments from its borrowers, and requiring internal and external audits.[34]

In 2004 and 2005, BlueOrchard, together with Developing World Markets Microfinance, LLC, a U.S.-based investment group, sold notes to individual and institutional investors, including the Omidyar Network, collateralized by MFO debt obligations. The investment vehicle, BlueOrchard Microfinance Securities 1, LLC, raised $86.5 million and financed fourteen MFOs in seven emerging nations with seven-year, fixed interest rate loans.[35] The MFOs' borrowings, the assets of the investment vehicle, serve as the collateral backing the issuance of senior and subordinated debt with different risk and return profiles. For investors, this structure allowed them to invest in a diversified portfolio of MFOs with a security that corresponded to their unique risk/return profile.

Securitization involves the bundling of loans, specifically, the debt obligations of MFOs, and selling them to investors in the form of bonds. The term "securitization" comes from turning an entity's loans to MFOs into bonds sold to investors. Securitization provides MFOs with access to capital at lower interest rates than they could obtain from local commercial banks.

The BlueOrchard deal is structured as a seven-year investment backed by MFO loans with a term of less than one year. The mismatch of the term between the bonds sold to investors and the collateral provided by the MFOs allows the MFOs to circulate funds to their borrowers several times before returning the principal to the investors.

With the BlueOrchard securitization backed by cash flows from uncollateralized loans to microentrepreneurs, the deal secured a $30 million guarantee from the Overseas Private Investment Corp. (OPIC), a U.S. government international development agency. OPIC's backing of a substantial part of the instruments issued to investors made that portion as safe as U.S. government obligations thereby facilitating the transaction.[36] Because the OPIC guarantee was so expensive, the buyers were foundations or institutions specializing in providing financing for microfinance and having aims, in part, that are philanthropic.

Omidyar Network also provided the lead investment in the Unitus Equity Fund, L.P., an international equity investment vehicle that targets a broad range of for-profit MFOs in Asia and Latin America. In 2006, Unitus, a nonprofit organization discussed in Chapter 3, created a separate entity, Unitus Equity Fund, L.P. (the Fund), a for-profit organization, to facilitate the development of a commercial equity market to serve the microfinance industry in Asia and Latin America. The Fund closed its first round of investments of $8.5 million in May 2006 and second round of some $15 million in March 2007. It is currently the largest global equity fund in the microfinance industry to be fully funded with private capital. Jim Bunch, the Omidyar Network's Director of Investments noted, "In working with the Fund over the past year, we have become even more convinced that it will play a catalytic role in helping scale microfinance while providing commercial-level returns for investors."[37] Ten percent of the Fund's profits go to Unitus to further its work to increase access to microfinance for the globe's working poor.

Nonprofit Microfinance Grants. Network's philanthropic arm has made numerous grants to nonprofits in the microfinance sector. The May 2006 donation to Unitus, Inc. by the Gates Foundation, discussed in Chapter 3, followed an earlier $2.7 million grant from Omidyar Network in September 2005 that enabled the nonprofit entity to expand its operations and hire key staff members. Doug Solomon (not a relative of the author), Omidyar Network's then vice president of investments, stated, "We share Unitus's belief that microfinance offers a sustainable and lasting solution for enabling the poor to lift themselves out of poverty through economic self-empowerment. With its focus on accelerating profitable growth and financial transparency among microfinance institutions, Unitus represents exactly the kind of organization Omidyar Network is eager to invest in."[38]

Unitus, which aims to demonstrate that MFOs can be run as large scale, poverty-focused, profit-making businesses, supports Omidyar's vision for the microfinance industry. It maintains that to grow to scale rapidly, MFOs need access to large amounts of capital to expand their operations and provide an array of financial products, such as offering savings deposits and various types of insurance, to many more clients. Only the formal, private capital markets, it asserts, can provide access to large quantities of the requisite capital. Conversely, MFOs that traditionally have relied on (and those that continue to rely on) donor dollars rarely have funds to develop their internal operating capacity with improvements in various areas, such as information technology, internal controls, human resources, and new products, thereby constricting their ability to create well-run operations and limiting their ability to grow on a sustainable basis. In short, both Unitus and Omidyar believe that commercial MFOs will demonstrate a more sustainable and scalable microfinance model than their nonprofit counterparts.[39]

Recognizing the importance of increased flows of accurate information in the microfinance sector, in 2005-2006 the Network provided a $1.5 million grant to the nonprofit Microfinance Information eXchange, Inc. (MIX). The funding enabled MIX to bring new technologies online and add staff in the areas of information technology and marketing.[40]

Launched in 2002, MIX, the Bloomberg of microfinance, has dedicated itself to improving the information infrastructure of the microfinance industry in the Third World by promoting standards of financial and operational reporting so as to standardize financial reporting across the sector, offering readily accessible data, and providing specialized information.[41] By providing a repository of reliable, comparable, and publicly available information on the financial strength and performance of MFOs, MIX provides an online information platform. Through the MIX Market, investors review and select the best performing MFOs to meet their investment needs. Client organizations can review and select intermediary organizations to meet their funding needs. Its efforts have helped accelerate the flow of information among more than eight hundred microfinance organizations worldwide.

The MIX Market follows a quality control system to help ensure the validity of its information. MFOs and investors verify the information they post, which the MIX Market then reviews for coherence and consistency. The MFOs and investors update their information in accordance with market standards, that is, annually or biannually. The MIX Market then ranks the levels of disclosure provided. The highest level indicates that an MFO has posted audited financial statements and adjusted data such as ratings or evaluations, shown due diligence, and reached other benchmarking assessments.

The Network also gave a $1.5 million grant in 2006 to the nonprofit International Development Law Organization, located in Rome, Italy, to train local attorneys and government policymakers to be more active in the development of the microfinance industry. The three-year training program will help build the capacity of the entire microfinance field. Among its other projects designed to promote the rule of law and good governance in developing countries, the organization works to facilitate the creation of statutes and regulations that support the growth of the microfinance industry.[42]

The Omidyar-Tufts University Microfinance Fund

In November 2005, the Omidyars gave $100 million to Tufts University to fund microenterprise ventures.[43] Although Pierre and Pamela, as alumni, had already made substantial contributions to Tufts, a new capital campaign was starting soon and the university's president was "circling." Omidyar recalled, "I was hearing, 'You're a pretty successful alumnus—you may have to step up.'"[44]

In late 2004, Pierre contacted Tufts University President Lawrence Bacow, an economist, to discuss how institutions could support investments in the microfinance field. Omidyar subsequently approached him with the idea of creating a microfinance fund. He emphasized that Tufts would receive some income from the investment vehicle, but it would also help create a new type of investment that would appeal to other institutions. The contribution would encourage entrepreneurship as a way to improve the economic status of individuals. According to Omidyar, "It's a fundamentally different way of looking at how to make a social impact. It's using business as a tool to make that happen."[45]

Instead of making a gift to the university's endowment and having the principal go into an investment pool with the donor directing that the return on capital go to a specific use, the Omidyars directed their entire contribution to the university go to support the microfinance mission. They gave $100 million in eBay shares to Tufts, the largest single gift in the university's history, but stipulated that the principal be dedicated to investments that would promote the commercialization of MFOs.

Omidyar insisted that the university create a separate fund for the gift to invest only in microfinance. With its own five person board of trustees, including Pierre and Tufts President Bacow, the Omidyar-Tufts Microfinance Fund, which is administered by the university, seeks to generate an annual return of at least 9 percent, a return in line with the rest of the university's endowment. Omidyar hoped the fund would serve as a "carrot," with microfinance organizations hungry for capital becoming more rigorous in the hope of becoming eligible for funding. The fund will test Omidyar's theories about the commercialization of the microfinance sector. It plans to be fully invested in three years, likely by late 2008.

The fund serves three purposes. First, it will demonstrate the potential of microfinance investments for institutional investors and thereby hopefully accelerate the growth of the sector. As Omidyar noted, "By connecting with an institutional investor like a university, we would like to increase the level of professional investor involvement in this sector to try to stimulate more commercially viable investment products,"[46] which would further open the access of MFOs to private capital markets.

Although Omidyar believes that there is a role for philanthropic capital in funding research and building microfinance infrastructure, he seeks to shrink the undemanding source of capital to MFOs contributed by donors who expect nothing in return and grow the demanding source of capital, which requires disclosure of material financial matters and offers an appropriate reward for the risk taken. As Tryfan Evans, the director of investments at the Omidyar-Tufts fund put it, "One of the things we need and we will get is a cycle of creative destruction."[47]

Second, the fund will support the Tufts University. Half of the income from the fund will go to the university, in an unrestricted manner, with the other half reinvested in the fund.

Third, when fully invested the fund itself could potentially stimulate at least $1 billion in new microloans over a decade. As Omidyar stated, "The social mission is to unleash at least $1 billion in microloans to the poor throughout the world over the next decade, as we make loans that are paid back and then recycled."[48]

The fund will invest directly and indirectly in microfinance organizations, but it will not lend directly to borrowers in developing countries. It will make direct investments in MFOs and indirect investments through MFIs that distribute funds to microfinance organizations. The fund will seek to diversify its investments across a number of dimensions: geography, currency, and investment fund managers. It will use six factors in making its investments: the strength of an organization; the quality of its people; the coherence of its investment philosophy and process; the prior performance achieved by the manager; the terms it is able to negotiate; and the fit of the product within the portfolio being developed.[49]

As one of its first investments, the Omidyar-Tufts Fund invested $8.6 million in ProCredit Holding AG, a Frankfurt, Germany for-profit bank holding company, led by C.P. Zeitinger, chairman of its supervisory board. The holding company's ownership structure, as it has evolved to its present form, consists of roughly equal groups of private sector and public sector shareholders, including national and international financial institutions, such as The World Bank Group's International Finance Corp.[50]

Zeitinger has built a network of nineteen banks in Eastern Europe, Latin America, and Africa. Planning to expand the network into Kyrgystan, Armenia, Sierra Leone, Colombia, Honduras and Mexico, he views his mission as creating financial institutions for "ordinary people," who lack access to the traditional financial system.

Each of the network's banks provides loans to microentrepreneurs and small business enterprises that previously did not have access to formal credit arrangements or were unattractive clients for mainstream commercial banks. Its for-profit model combines a commercial approach with a development policy orientation, giving ProCredit a stable future. In addition to its core business of micro- and small business loans, the network's platform offers a number of other financial services for its banks' customers, including savings deposit facilities, domestic and international payments, credit cards, and home improvement loans. It uses a lending methodology combining a careful analysis of credit risks, such as avoiding business startups, with a high degree of standardization requisite for efficiency and outreach to a large number of small borrowers. Unlike traditional MFOs, such as Pro Mujer, its banks provide individual, not group, loans. Borrowers also come to its banks to repay their loans.[51]

Zeitinger, who wants to obtain more grant money to expand into harder-to-serve rural regions, avoids denigrating philanthropic donations. In building the ProCredit bank network, he obtained grants and loans from national and international development agencies. Even now, when it opens a bank in a new country, ProCredit accepts subsidies and donations for the first two or three years, when it faces high start-up costs and little revenue. Thus, Zeitinger characterizes Omidyar's resistance to the use of grant money by MFOs as "naïve."[52] Zeitinger believes there needs to be more MFOs, but new ones cannot emerge on their own; they require donations and public sector subsidies in order to get started. He does not believe that the microfinance sector will one day become completely self-sustaining. According to him, philanthropic, nongovernmental organizations, and governmental funding on some level will always be required to keep the sector running.

Some Observations Regarding Microfinance Organizations and Microfinance Institutions

Omidyar has put his faith in the ability of for-profit businesses to achieve socially beneficial outcomes through microfinance lending. His multi-faceted approach has put him on a different path than some other big names in the microfinance world, including Yunus. Additionally, it is far too early to tell whether microfinance will achieve the lofty goals it has set for itself, with or without philanthropic donations. There are many potential obstacles on the horizon.

For instance, it may be difficult for Omidyar Network and the Omidyar-Tufts Fund to find suitable investments. The relative youth of the microfinance sector means that there currently exist only a limited number of large-scale MCOs and MFOs with the potential for sustainability. To invest on the scale Omidyar expects of the Omidyar-Tufts Fund and the Network, more larger MCOs and MFOs need to emerge.

There are additional risks that come with doing business in a global market. MFIs generally lend in hard currency, but MCOs and MFOs lend in local currencies. To a large extent, exchange rates and the stability of local markets may dictate the return investors get. This is a particular problem in the world of microfinance because MCOs and MFOs generally operate in some of the world's poorest countries, where governments are often corrupt and less likely to be stable. Such risks may make microfinance too risky for some investors, whose primary goal is a predictable rate of return rather than philanthropy.

An absorptive capacity problem exists. Large, sustainable MCOs and MFOs already have access to local capital from commercial banks, but there are not enough such organizations to fulfill Omidyar's vision of economic self-empowerment. Most MCOs and MFOs, however, are too small to use additional funds effectively, so donations and investments do not go as far. The result is a dilemma for foundations and investors as well as the need to build organizations up to the point where they can use donations and investments efficiently. To minimize MFIs's transaction costs, large numbers of formally-rated microfinance organizations may need to combine in some way. Money apart, MCOs and MFOs also need talented people to work for them, particularly as programs grow to a larger scale, customers will require more services, such as savings accounts, insurance, and mortgages.

Finally, the 2007-2008 global crunch, triggered by risky mortgages in the United States, presents an additional dilemma. The securitization doldrums began in mid-2007, as rising defaults by U.S. subprime home buyers rattled the debt market. As banks struggled to clean up their balance sheets and investors hesitated to buy packages of debt sliced into pieces (so-called tranches) the funding of MFIs, such as BlueOrchard Finance, came to a halt, at least temporarily.

It is currently too early to tell whether Omidyar's vision of a large scale, self-sufficient, social mission microfinance sector will play out, or whether Yunus is correct in emphasizing the purely philanthropic nature of the effort. Because the problems of poverty alleviation are deep and intractable, the answer may still be years away. However, the regulated, for-profit status of MFOs offers many benefits. Regulation and regular supervision by national authorities increase an MFO's internal discipline and facilitate greater confidence in its operations. In many countries, regulation allows MFOs to expand their product offerings to include savings products, which are often more popular than microloans. Regulated MFOs can mobilize savings as a source of funds for lending at lower interest rates than borrowing from local banks. For-profit status for an MFO also helps clarify its board's financial responsibility, enabling commercial banks and potential private investors to see clearly who sets policy for the entity. The governance role provided by an MFO's board of directors will likely make it easier for the organization to access a broader range of financing options, including both equity investments and debt funding. Capital invested in the form of equity provides a cushion and increases the likelihood that an MFO will be able to repay its loans even if its operations fail to meet expectations, thereby heightening the confidence of lenders, such as local commercial banks. Increasing an MFO's access to sources of long-term funds reduces an entity's dependency on donated funds and permits an institution to develop more long-term, stable financial relationships with private capital market institutions having a greater capacity to meet the financial needs of a growing, sustainable organization.[53]

Through Omidyar Network and the Omidyar-Tufts University Microfinance Fund, Pierre Omidyar seeks to align strategic philanthropy with socially responsible investing and grant-making to create sustainable, scalable for-profit businesses and nonprofit entities, having a social impact. If successful, Omidyar will have started his career by revolutionizing the way people do business over the Internet, and in a second act change philanthropy forever.

Notes

1. Matthew Miller, "The Forbes 400," *Forbes* 178:7 (October 8, 2007): 72-326, at 158.
2. Luisa Kroll with Matthew Miller, "The Billionaire Rankings: Index," *Forbes* 181:6 (March 24, 2008): 146-160, at 156.
3. For background on Pierre Omidyar I have drawn on: Adam Cohen, *The Perfect Store: Inside eBay* (Boston: Little, Brown & Co., 2002); Adam Cohen, "Pierre Omidyar's Perfect Store Turns 10," *New York Times*, September 7, 2005, A24; Brad Kelly, "Omidyar Bid Right With eBay," *Investor's Business Daily*, January 22, 2007, A4.
4. Tufts University, "Profile: About Tufts" <*http://www.tufts. edu/home/about/ ?p=profile*> (July 5, 2007).
5. Peter Newcomb, "The Ranking," *Forbes* 164:9 (October 11, 1999): 414-418, at 414.
6. Erika Brown, "What Would Meg Do?" *Forbes* 179:11 (May 21, 2007): 94-100, at 96.
7. Catherine Holahan, "Going, Going ... Everywhere," *BusinessWeek* 4039 (June 18, 2007): 62-64.
8. eBay Inc., U.S. Securities and Exchange Commission Form 10-K, February 28, 2007, 1.
9. The quotations and the statistics are from Connie Bruck, "Millions for Millions," *New Yorker* 82:35 (October 30, 2006): 62-73, at 68.
10. Stephanie Strom, "What's Wrong with Profit?" *New York Times*, November 13, 2006, F1.
11. Karen Breslau, "Family Foundation," in "The Giving Back Awards," *Newsweek* 148:1-2 (July 10, 2006): 55-86, at 57.
12. Bill Breen, "Q & A: Pierre Omidyar—Empower Seller," *Fast Company* 113 (March 2007): 89 <*http://www.fastcompany.com/magazine /113*> (March 16, 2007); Robert D. Hof, "Doing Good—and Making Money, Too," *BusinessWeek* 3877 (April 5, 2004): 14.
13. Michelle Conlin with Rob Hof, "The eBay Way," *BusinessWeek* 3910 (November 29, 2004): 96-98, at 96.
14. Omidyar Network, "About" <*http://www.omidyar.net/about.php*> (April 9, 2008). For background on the Omidyar Network have drawn on: Conlin with Hof, "The eBay Way;" Nicole Wallace, "Blending Business and Charity," *Chronicle of Philanthropy* 18:24 (September 28, 2006): 14-15; Peter Karoff with Jane Maddox, *The World We Want: New Dimensions in Philanthropy and Social Change* (Lanham, MD: AltaMira, 2007), 35-44.
15. David Kirkpatrick, "ebay's Founder Starts Giving," *Fortune* 152:11 (November 28, 2005): 49.
16. Karen W. Arenson, "Tufts Is Getting Gift of $100 Million with Rare Strings," *New York Times*, November 4, 2005, A16.
17. Douglas McGray, "Network Philanthropy," *West (Los Angeles Times)*, January 21, 2007, 14-17, 31-36, at 32.
18. Omidyar Network, "About" <*http://www.omidyar.net/about.php*> (April 9, 2008). See also George Anders, "ebay's Founder Bets on 'Participatory Media,'" *Wall Street Journal*, October 17, 2007, A2.

19. Breen, "Q & A," 89.
20. DonorsChoose, "How It Works" <http://www.donorschoose.org/about.html> (April 18, 2007); DonorsChoose, Inc., Financial Statements and Additional Information, June 30, 2006 and 2005, Note 8 to Financial Statements; Omidyar Network Fund, Inc., 2005 Internal Revenue Service Form 990-PF, Statement 12. See also Kirk Shinkle, "Best Shot At Helping Students," *Investor's Business Daily*, December 20, 2006, A4; Stephanie Banchero, "Web site for donors a goldmine for schools," *Chicago Tribune*, January 22, 2007, 1; Tamar Lewin, "Building Better Schools, One Glue Stick at a Time," *New York Times*, November 14, 2005, F14; Erika Hayasaki, "Website Provides Direct Hookup Between Schools and Donors," *Los Angeles Times*, October 27, 2005, B6; Stephanie Strom, "Prize To Group That Uses Web To Aid Schools," *New York Times*, October 12, 2005, C9; Jessi Hempel, "It Takes A Web Site," *BusinessWeek* 3952 (September 26, 2005): 88-90; Hope Reeves, "From a Young Teacher, a Way to Get Donors for Class Projects," *New York Times*, December 24, 2003, B8; Stephanie Strom, "Matching Givers With Those In Need," *New York Times*, July 2, 2002, B1.
21. DonorsChoose, "Our Story and Mission" <http://www.donors choose.org/about/history.html> (April 18, 2007).
22. Omidyar Network, "Portfolio" <http://home.omidyar.net/portfolio.php> (April 9, 2008).
23. Email, Kelly Mason, Manager Communications, Omidyar Network, to Lewis D. Solomon, April 9, 2008.
24. Prosper Marketplace Inc. (Prosper), "Company Overview" <http://www.prosper.com/about> (April 17, 2007); Prosper, "How It Works" <http://www.prosper.com/welcome/how_it_works.aspx> (April 17, 2007); Prosper, "Fees" <http://www.prosper.com/welcome/fees.aspx> (April 17, 2007); Prosper, Press Release, "Prosper Secures an Additional $20 Million," June 30, 2007. See also Michael Sisk, "The Rise of Community," *Bank Technology News* 20:12 (December 2007): 30-33; Breen, "Q & A," 89; Jane J. Kim, "Options Grow For Investors To Lend Online," *Wall Street Journal* (July 18, 2007): D1; Jonathan V. Last, "Usury for Beginners," *Wall Street Journal* (April 6, 2007): W11; Charles Davis, "Cutting Out Banks Altogether," *Retail Banker International* 570 (April 18, 2007): 6; Anne Kadet, "The Banker Next Door," *SmartMoney* 16:4 (April 2007): 92-97; Christopher Steiner, "The ebay of Loans," *Forbes* 179:5 (March 12, 2007): 68-70; Annys Shin, "Want To Loan Me Money? Here's a Picture of My Dog," *Washington Post* (January 27, 2007): D1; Loren Fox, "The Kindness of Strangers," *Institutional Investor* (International Edition) 31:7 (September 2006): 201-204; Timothy J. Mullaney, "Lots of Loans, But No Banks," *BusinessWeek* 3991 (July 3, 2006): 72-73; Carolyn Said, "Site Hooks up Lenders, Borrowers," *San Francisco Chronicle* (March 6, 2006): C1; Bob Tedeschi, "It's Like Lending to a Friend, Except You'll Get Interest," *New York Times* (February 13, 2006): C1.
25. Kadet, "Banker Next Door," 94.
26. Omidyar Network, "Portfolio."
27. Pierre Omidyar, "A Pro-Poor Investment Strategy: Capital, Innovation and the Market," *Clinton Global Initiative Conference* (September 16, 2005): 6.
28. Fergal Byne, "Auction Man," *Financial Times Weekend Magazine* (London), (March 25, 2006): 16.
29. Robert Hof, "Tiny Investments, Big Changes," *BusinessWeek Online*, November 4, 2005 <http://www.businessweek.com/technology/content/nov2005/tc20051104_079665.htm>, (November 7, 2006). See also Jay Green, "Taking Tiny Loans to the Next Level," *BusinessWeek* 4011 (November 27, 2006): 76-79, at 79.

30. Bruck, "Millions," 64.
31. Muhammad Yunus (with Alan Jolis) traces the development of his microlending program in *Banker To The Poor: Micro-Lending and the Battle Against World Poverty* (New York: PublicAffairs, 1999) and Muhammad Yunus with Karl Weber, *Creating a World Without Poverty: Social Business and the Future of Capitalism* (New York: PublicAffairs, 2007), 43-75. For background on Yunus see Cecilia W. Dugger, "Peace Prize to Pioneer of Loans For Those Too Poor to Borrow," *New York Times* (October 14, 2006): A1; Molly Moore, "Micro-Credit Pioneer Wins Peace Prize," *Washington Post* (October 14, 2006): A1; Michael M. Phillips, Marcus Walker, Mark Whitehouse, "'Microloan' Father Yunus Is Awarded Nobel Peace Prize," *Wall Street Journal* (October 14-15, 2006): B1; Jesse Emspak, "Muhammad Yunus' Nobel Cause In Bangladesh," *Investor's Business Daily*, May 23, 2007, A3.
32. Bruck, "Millions," 64.
33. The quotations in this paragraph are from Bruck, "Millions," 64. See also Karoff with Maddox, *World We Want*, 40-41 and Andrew Curry, "Why Nobel laureate Mohammad Yunus will doom microfinance," *New Republic Online*, December 7, 2006 <www.tnr.com/doc.mhtml?i=w0612 04&s=curry120706>.
34. BlueOrchard Finance S.A., "Home/About Us/Who we are" <http://www.blueorchard.org/jahia/Jahia/pid/8> (April 13, 2007). See also Chris Dammers, "Microfinance CDO brings funds to poor," *Euroweek*, March 3, 2006, 1; Harry Hurt III, "A Path to Helping the Poor and His Investors," *New York Times*, August 10, 2003, Section 3, 4; Francesca Sears, "Banking the Unbankable," *Forbes Global* 5:11 (May 27, 2002): 74.
35. Blue Orchard Microfinance Securities 1, LLC, "Fact Sheet" <http://www.blueorchard.org/jahia/webdav/site/blueorchard/shared/Products/BOMS1/BOMS1_FactSheet_20050627.pdf> (September 13, 2006); The MIXMarket, "BlueOrchard Microfinance Securities 1 (Fund)" <http://www.mixmarket.org/en/supply/supply.show.profile.asp?>(January 7, 2007). See also Grameen Foundation USA, *Tapping Financial Markets for Microfinance*, February 2005, 12. In 2006 and 2007, BlueOrchard vehicles raised $106 million and $108 million, respectively. The 2007 deal, packaged as a collaterized loan obligation, with four tranches offering different degrees of risk and return, marked the first time a securitized microfinance deal achieved a credit rating, which opened the debt to a broader range of investors. Paul J. Davies, "Rating Opens Door to Altruistic Microfinancing," *Financial Times* (London), May 10, 2007, 43; Samantha Rowan, "Blue Orchard Loans for Development 2006-1," *Journal of Structured Finance* 12:1 (March 22, 2006): 123; Paul J. Davies, "Bond Gives Boost to Microfinance," *Financial Times* (London), March 2, 2006, 8; Paul J. Davies, "Public Deal Lifts 'Micro' Initiative," *Financial Times* (London) April 13, 1006, 41.
36. Elizabeth Wine, "Pooling Resources," *Worth* 14:4 (April 2005): 110-113, at 111, 113.
37. Unitus Equity Fund L.P. (Unitus Equity Fund), Press Release, "Unitus Equity Fund Closes Largest Private Global Equity Fund Targeting Microfinance," March 26, 2007. See also Kristi Heim, "Making a Profit while Helping the Poor," *Seattle Times* (April 29, 2007): A1; Alexander Haislip, "Nonprofit Launches $35m Microfinance Fund," *Private Equity Week* 13:35 (September 11, 2006): 1; Unitus Equity Fund, Press Release, "Unitus Equity Fund Appoints Chris Brookfield Investment Director and Announces First Major Microfinance Investments in India," May 22, 2006; Tricia Duryee, "Microfinance gets VC nudge," *Seattle Times* (May 22, 2006): E1.

38. Unitus, Inc. (Unitus), Press Release, "Unitus Announces $2.7 Grant From Omidyar Network," September 30, 2005.
39. Unitus, "Industry Problem: Supply Not Meeting Demand" <http://www.unitus.com/sections/poverty/poverty_ip_main.asp> (December 18, 2006).
40. The Microfinance Information Exchange, Press Release, "The MIX receives funding from Omidyar Network," November 20, 2005 and The Microfinance Information Exchange, Press Release, "MIX Receives Second-Tranche of Investment from Omidyar Network," May 18, 2006. See also Greene, "Taking Tiny Loans."
41. The MIXMarket, "Welcome to the MIXMarket!" <http://www.mixmarket.org/en/about_mix_market.asp> (March 21, 2007); The MIXMarket, "About the MIX" <http://www.mixmarket.org/en/what.is.mix.asp> (March 21, 2007).
42. International Development Law Organization, Press Release, "IDLO receives US $1.5 million for Microfinance Program from Omidyar Network, July 20, 2006. See also Wallace, "Blending Business and Charity."
43. Tufts University, Press Release, "eBay and Omidyar Network Founder Launches $100 Million Fund in Partnership with Tufts University," November 4, 2005. I have also drawn on Paul Fain, "Tufts U. to Use $100-Million Gift to Make Microloans in Developing Countries," *Chronicle of Philanthropy* 18:4 (November 24, 2005): 20; Rob Hof, "A Big Fund For Tiny Businesses," *BusinessWeek* 3959 (November 14, 2005): 13; Robert Hof, "Tiny Investments;" Mylene Mangalinda and Elizabeth Bernstein, "An eBay Founder's Bid to Aid the Poor," *Wall Street Journal* (November 4, 2005): W1; Dan Roberts, "Founder of eBay Sets up Dollars 100m Microfinance Aid Fund," *Financial Times* (London), November 4, 2005, 8; Arenson, "Tufts Is Getting Gift of $100 Million"; Jim Hopkins, "He's Donating $10 Million to a University," *USA Today* (November 4, 2005): 1B; Jim Hopkins, "Tufts Does Well while Doing Good," *USA Today* (November 4, 2005): 2B.
44. Bruck, "Millions," 64.
45. Mangalinda and Bernstein, "eBay Founder's Bid."
46. Hof, "Tiny Investments."
47. Bruck, "Millions," 70.
48. Kirkpatrick, "Ebay's Founder."
49. Marc Raifman, "Tufts Takes Steps to Invest Omidyar Microfinance Fund," *Tufts Daily*, May 21, 2006 <www.tuftsdaily.com> (March 21, 2007).
50. ProCredit Holding, Press Release "Significant Capital Increase at ProCredit Holding AG," September 19, 2006 and ProCredit Holding, "Managers and Owners" <http://www.procredit-holding.com/csm/front_content.php?>(April 13, 2007).
51. ProCredit Holding, "Introduction," Business Philosophy," and "ProCredit Institutions," <http://www.procredit-holding.com/cms/ front_content.php?> (April 13, 2007); C.P. Zeitinger, "ProCredit Holding: Where We Are Today," *ProCredit Holding News* (January 2006): 6-9. See also, The MIXMarket, "ProCredit Holding AG" <http://www.mixmarket.org> (January 7, 2007); Andrew Curry, "Microcredit finds its European niche," *Christian Science Monitor* (November 13, 2006): 7; *Economist*, "From Charity to Business," 377:8451 (November 5, 2005): 6-8; Gabriele Heber, interview by Hans Dembowski, "Prime Example of Pro-Poor Growth," *D+C Magazine* 33 (2006:1) 18-20.
52. Bruck, "Millions," 72.
53. Unitus, "Our Goals: MFI Transformation," <http://www.unitus.com/sections/aboutus/aboutus_os_goals.asp> (December 20, 2006).

5

Jeffrey Skoll and His Philanthropic Endeavors: Funding Social Entrepreneurs and Motion Pictures

Jeffrey Skoll made his fortune as an entrepreneurially-oriented business executive. In March 2008, with 8 percent of eBay's stock, *Forbes* estimated his net worth at $3.6 billion, placing him at number 296 among the world's 1,125 billionaires.[1] It only makes sense, then, that he would use part of fortune to support other entrepreneurs.

Since 1999, Skoll has sought to advance the effectiveness of social entrepreneurs, as social change agents, through his philanthropy. To advance social causes, he has also engaged in a for-profit film industry venture through his company, Participant Productions.

Skoll, a tough-minded optimist, believes in the possibility of change and progress. He recalled a rich friend who had retired to play golf and enjoy life. His friend stated, "Well, I think the world's in terrible shape and so I just want to have a good time, take care of my family, enjoy my friends, and that's it." Skoll inquired, "How can you feel that way if you really love your kids? Don't you want to make the world better for them?" The friend replied, "Well, take the Middle East. If you can show me there's any hope of resolving that, maybe." In the spring of 2005, Skoll had the movie "Gandhi" dubbed into Arabic and started hosting screenings in Palestinian refugee camps with the ultimate objective of having one million Arabs learn about a nonviolence hero. Skoll recalled, "My same friend saw that project, and he decided to help out and do something with my foundation."[2]

Skoll looks at his post-eBay endeavors in an integrated way: argument and entertainment and entrepreneurship; nonprofit and for-profit and breakeven. The Skoll Foundation's chief operating officer, Richard Fahey, sums up the diversity and convergence: "We have the view that our capital is a continuum."³ The idea is that government and private donors must work together to support change-makers. Skoll stated, "I believe innovation comes when a group of people at the grassroots level get it in their heads that they want to improve things. Then, the government acts in concert with them to make that happen."⁴

Skoll's primary objective in his philanthropy is not to make money, nor does he even truly care if the organizations to which his foundation donates break even, as his eBay business partner, Pierre Omidyar, does. Rather, Skoll is interested in increasing the collective social consciousness and alleviating what he sees as the unforgivable wealth disparities in the world. He has used both a nonprofit foundation and a for-profit media company to advance his goal of ending the gap between the haves and the have nots. His philanthropy has focused primarily on discovering the most effective way of solving this root problem. For Skoll, that quest led him to focus on social entrepreneurship in a number of different forms.

Background on Jeffrey Skoll

Jeffrey Skoll was born in 1965. Growing up in Montreal in the 1970s, he worried about the world. "Politics, the environment, overpopulation—the future seemed very scary," Skoll recalled,⁵ absorbing the prevailing North American cultural left's pessimistic outlook.

According to Skoll, "My family camped in upstate New York and there wasn't a lot to do. So I would read—books like *Brave New World* and *1984*, [authors like] Ayn Rand and James Michener—and it just struck me that the future was looking pretty scary. It also seemed that a lot of problems derived from inequities between rich and poor. I wanted to make a difference in that equation."⁶

Sensitive and serious as a teenager, he thought about becoming a crusading writer who would explore various social problems and promote concrete solutions. For Skoll, "All these books made the world seem a very small place, very interconnected. Around the same time, I became conscious of all these scary things happening in the world: overpopulation, nuclear war, and global warming and that the future may not be a very pleasant place. And I thought, wouldn't it be great to write stories that made people see these problems that were coming and got people involved before they actually happened."⁷

Then pragmatism set in. Skoll realized he needed to make enough money to take time off to write. Realizing that writing would not pay the bills, he received a bachelor's degree in electrical engineering at the

University of Toronto. After graduating in 1987, he launched an engineering consulting firm that helped clients set up inventory management and accounting systems; he also ran a computer rental company, Micros on the Move, Ltd.

Grasping how little he knew about business and that he needed more business knowledge if his enterprises were to grow, he went west and received an MBA at Stanford University in 1995. Skoll indicated, "I wanted to be a writer, to write these stories that would make people see the world in a different way. But I ended up going to business school because I thought I could ultimately get to where I wanted to go faster that way."[8]

After graduating from Stanford, Skoll became attracted to the Internet's potential and took a job at Knight-Ridder Information, Inc., part of the newspaper conglomerate. It was when he was working here that Pierre Omidyar first approached him with the idea of helping him with AuctionWeb, an online auction site Omidyar had developed that would soon become eBay.

Skoll, Omidyar, and eBay

In Silicon Valley, Skoll met Omidyar in 1994 through a mutual friend while still getting his MBA at Stanford.[9] After they clicked on a personal level, Omidyar introduced him to the eBay concept in the fall of 1995. At first, Skoll told Omidyar "it was a stupid idea,"[10] but then agreed to come on board.

Skoll and Omidyar turned out to be a dynamic team. Omidyar had always been a dreamer. With Skoll he got someone who put those dreams into practice. "It was the perfect balance," Omidyar said. "I tended to think more intuitively, and he could say, 'Okay, let's see how we can actually get that done.'"[11] When Omidyar decided his auction website should grow to scale, it only made sense that he asked Skoll to draw up a business plan for what would become eBay. Skoll became the company's first president, stepping aside when Margaret (Meg) Whitman became CEO in 1998.

Similar to Omidyar, Skoll saw eBay as having a social mission. Skoll recalled, "From the very start, the success of the community was the success of the company. One of the things that we were most proud of was that there were people who were buying and selling on eBay that substantially improved their lives. They had access to a level playing field, something they ... never had before. Single mothers were able to stay at home with their kids and make a living, disabled folks were able to make a living. Seniors who couldn't get around too well, could make a living...."[12] As a grassroots organization, Skoll noted, "It [eBay] was a vehicle that allowed people to become empowered and communicate with each other. It was hard to tell where the company left off and the community began."[13]

Once the company got off the ground, Skoll focused eBay on corporate philanthropy. He stated, "There was a recognition in the genes of the company of the importance of giving back to the community as the company grew. It led to the eBay Foundation which was unique at the time [1998]. It was the first foundation created with pre-IPO stock. It took a little bit of work to make happen, but once we did it became a model that other companies have since followed."[14]

By 2000, about two and a half years after eBay went public, Skoll felt comfortable that the management team led by CEO Meg Whitman could handle the business without his being there. At age 36, in 2001, he retired from eBay. Until that point, he was reluctant to let go of his institutional memory function, whether in terms of some knowledge, or value, of the way eBay worked. Once he felt that the senior management team had absorbed the founders' values, especially the "importance of that community-company synergy and the values that held it together," Skoll felt "comfortable moving on to start pursuing the dream I had of making a difference to the equation of inequities."[15]

Skoll's Personal Philanthropy

Skoll's philanthropic drive stems from two sources—a disgust of what he regards as the prevailing inequalities and a feeling that conventional methods of combating it are ineffective. According to Skoll, "There is a [realization] that traditional political or business approaches have not eliminated the problems of the world. We're living in a fragile house of cards that could come down at any time."[16]

Skoll is appalled by the extremes of wealth and poverty in the United States and, more generally, globally. He indicated, "Having grown up in Canada, I saw that there was a better way and people don't have to fall through the cracks. There is no reason why there should be such desperation among people living in a wealthy country." Similar to Gates, his philanthropy strives, in large part, to deal with the sources of inequality. For Skoll, "I think everything from crime to disease to terrorism really has its roots in the fact that there are people who are really desperate."[17]

Despite a clear goal, however, Skoll's initial philanthropic endeavors were rather unfocused and inefficient. In 1999, before leaving eBay, he created: the Skoll Community Fund, a tax exempt supporting organization associated with a community foundation; the Silicon Valley Community Foundation (SVCF), formerly the Community Foundation Silicon Valley. A supporting organization is a public charity qualifying under Section 509(a)(3) of the Internal Revenue Code for special benefits and advantageous treatment not available to private foundations. Contributions to a supporting organization qualify for the highest federal income tax deductibility thresholds, specifically, for individuals, 50 percent of adjusted gross income for cash contributions, and 30 percent for gifts of appreciated assets.[18] The SVCF, as the Skoll Community Fund's legal sponsor, maintains fiduciary control over its affairs, primarily by appointing a majority of its directors.

Grant-making by the Skoll Community Fund began in early 2000 in eight broad areas: children, families, and communities; health, education, and science; the environment; and technology. Then in 2001, focusing on the themes of empowerment, community, and impact, it developed its mission statement. Its eight initial funding areas became four: learning and education; philanthropy; microenterprise; and technology.[19]

Since its establishment in 2002, Skoll's main focus has been the Skoll Foundation. He has invested over $600 million and much of his time into his foundation, but only recently he seemed to have found its true purpose, committing some $100 million to social entrepreneurs.

After nearly five years of earnest, but rather unfocused, charitable giving, in 2004 Skoll brought in consultants to hone his philanthropic efforts and the foundation's brand. He came to realize that the nonprofits he admired needed: longer term funding than traditional foundations offered; more flexibility in using donated funds; a funder to partner with them and brainstorm how to measure success; and help in getting their message to a wider audience. Armed with new graphics, a tighter slogan, and a new purpose, Skoll and the foundation's staff came to focus about 60 percent of its annual grants on social entrepreneurship, not social service agencies.[20] Its mission now centers on advancing "systemic change to benefit communities around the world by investing in, connecting and celebrating social entrepreneurs."[21] About 25 percent of its annual grants help build the capacity of organizations serving the entire nonprofit sector, with 15 percent allocated to nonprofit groups working in Silicon Valley.[22]

For Skoll, social entrepreneurs serve as "society's change agents: the pioneers of innovation for the social sector." Similar to business entrepreneurs, social entrepreneurs "see and act on what others miss, the opportunities to improve systems, to create solutions, to invent new approaches." Unlike business entrepreneurs, who "go after a problem from a purely economic viewpoint, social entrepreneurs usually have a vision of something that they would like to solve in the social sector. They are not necessarily in it for personal materialistic or monetary remuneration."[23] In short, social entrepreneurs operate nonprofit ventures aiming to contribute to the betterment of society; they strive to find innovative ways to meet human needs that go unmet by either the public or private sectors.[24]

"But more people now [realize] and [recognize] that the social ills around the world are not going away and that traditional approaches (to these problems) won't work," Skoll stated. "I think social entrepreneurs [recognize] this, and they are dedicating their time and their talents to solving these social ills. I think their success will determine how well we advance as a species over the next century."[25]

The foundation provides funding to existing, small, social entrepreneurial entities that are ready to grow. In other words, it targets ventures that are scalable and need capital to take their idea to the next level. It identifies nonprofits with ideas capable of transforming a political, social or economic market, gives them three years of capital to go from local to regional, or regional to national, and thus achieve scale. It seeks out organizations that already have a well-developed sense of what they want to achieve, clear early success, and a realistic plan to get there. In short, it tries to identify great nonprofits and helps them amplify their impact.

More specifically, the foundation uses four analytical factors in deciding to make a contribution to a social entrepreneur. First, what is the entrepreneurial quality of the idea? Is it innovative? How much of a breakthrough is there? Is it designed to effect systemic change? Second, it looks for traction. It does not generally fund early stage social entrepreneurs, looking instead to fund the expansion of proven projects. It wants those who already have a viable program, which is on its way to effecting systemic change. It asks: is the social entrepreneur with a world-changing idea, who is doing it in a small way, ready to take it out regionally or globally? Third, what is the organization's capacity? It looks at how a social entrepreneur is building the capacity to drive his or her innovation forward. It searches for an institution, a group of people, and a base of resources behind an innovation. Finally, it focuses on integrity. It wants people who walk their talk, who are dedicated, have the power of their convictions, and who know how to mobilize and inspire others to join them. In the final analysis, it asks: does someone ring true; is he or she an effective nonprofit leader?[26]

The foundation funds social entrepreneurial innovators, through the annual Skoll Awards for Social Entrepreneurship, who are tackling the world's biggest problems, from housing AIDS orphans in Africa to developing new pharmaceuticals for infectious diseases, with a scalable approach capable of bring lasting change to society. With its focus on social entrepreneurs, it diversifies its funding globally through different sectors in which social entrepreneurs work. The foundation designed the awards, as three-year grants, to advance solutions to critical social problems and recognize programs generating positive social change in the areas of: tolerance and human rights; health; environmental sustainability; peace and security; institutional responsibility; and economic and social equity.

Funding Social Entrepreneurs

The Skoll Foundation has empowered a variety of social entrepreneurs "to extend their reach, deepen their impact and fundamentally improve society."[27] Among the numerous social entrepreneurs the foundation has funded, this section examines four organizations: Acumen Fund; Institute for OneWorld Health; Benetech; and KickStart.

The Skoll Foundation has donated to the Acumen Fund Inc., a nonprofit venture capital fund, founded in 2001 with seed money and advice from the Rockefeller Foundation, Cisco Systems Foundation, and the three individual philanthropists.[28] In financing third-world companies, Acumen has created a laboratory for designing new business models and funding techniques.

As refined over the years, Acumen's investments consist of three portfolios: health, water, and housing.[29] Its health portfolio focuses on investing in technologies and associated business systems that increase the quality of and access to healthcare. It makes investments in infrastructure and financing systems to help make home ownership more accessible. To improve the quality and availability of fresh water supplies, it invests in purification, distribution, and conservation solutions. It incurs high risks in providing capital to businesses that focus on low-income markets without necessarily looking for high returns.

The Acumen Fund seeks to build prototypes for new businesses that measure returns in both social benefits and monetary rewards. It evaluates new projects for their social impact, financial sustainability, replicability, and breakthrough insights that can be applied elsewhere. Using its managerial and entrepreneurial expertise, Acumen strives to create a template for how businesses can provide affordable, critical goods and services in its three areas of interest to poor people in developing nations. The design fundamentals Acumen uses in its work are four-fold: observing customers to uncover their unmet needs; helping firms create prototypes of new products and services for customers; integrating those goods and services until they work; and looking for new business models.

Acumen leverages the charitable funds it receives by making equity and debt investments in businesses, not through grants to these firms. It found that grants did not provide firms with the same type of financial discipline or serve as a conduit into more traditional financial markets.

The three-year $1.5 million partnership between the Skoll Foundation and Acumen provided new opportunities to leverage the foundation's and Acumen's complementary knowledge, skills, and assets. The foundation's support enabled Acumen to develop metrics that advanced the understanding of the financial and social impact of a specific type of social business. The goal of the partnership centered on identifying high-performing, for-profit social enterprises and attempting to quantify the impact of these enterprises in alleviating poverty, as opposed to a purely charitable model. Similar to Omidyar's microfinance endeavors, analyzed in Chapter 4, the partnership sought to test whether an entrepreneurial model is more sustainable than a charitable one.[30]

The Institute for OneWorld Health, the world's first nonprofit pharmaceutical company, runs clinical trials and brings to market drugs for diseases in the Third World.[31] In striving to assure a more equitable treatment of diseases afflicting the world's poor, OneWorld Health has brought previously developed drugs to markets that big companies saw as unprofitable—such as an antibiotic that now helps to fight "black fever" in India—and also works to develop its own pharmaceutical solutions to Third World diseases, such as malaria and diarrhea. The Institute has obtained grants from foundations, including $615,000 from the Skoll Foundation as well as major support from the Gates Foundation.[32] It used the Skoll funds to develop its managerial infrastructure. Thus, OneWorld Health has positioned itself to bring First World money to Third World problems with the understanding that most of the diseases it is fighting may be curable at a low cost to the poor who fall ill.

Benetech (more formally, Beneficent Technology, Inc.), a nonprofit entity, takes existing technology and creates new uses for it that have a social benefit.[33] It works in two major areas: literacy and human rights. Benetech developed Bookshare, the world's largest digital library of scanned text materials for the visually impaired. *Bookshare.org*'s online library delivers accessible books over the Internet. A user can listen to a digital book on a personal computer with voice synthesizer software or load it into a Braille display for portable reading. It also created software to monitor and document human rights abuses. For grassroots activists, it created a simple, secure software application for gathering, organizing, and backing up documentation of human rights abuses.

Benetech's business model resembles a start-up funded by venture capital, with the returns on investment measured by the number of people it serves, not profits. The firm plows back money it makes to seed more projects.

For the Skoll Foundation, Benetech's appeal thus turned on the promise of a high social yield on each dollar contributed. The foundation awarded Benetech, which is also funded by the Omidyar Network, a three-year grant of $1,215,000 to expand its existing programs and create new projects.[34]

The Skoll Foundation has supported KickStart International, Inc., a nonprofit organization that designs and develops low-technology agricultural machines.[35] Its human powered, low-tech agricultural equipment helps poor African farmers make their land more productive. For example, its two types of irrigation pumps sell for $80 and $40 and are made by small manufacturers trained by KickStart and sold by retailers to farmers. Using a water pump, a farmer can irrigate more land in the dry season and cultivate profitable fruits and vegetables to generate cash, thereby "kickstarting" family wealth and economic growth. The foundation's three-year grant of $615,000 allowed KickStart to strengthen its operations (including leasing an office in San Francisco from which it can do fundraising), develop two new products, and reach 50,000 more clients.[36]

Connecting Social Entrepreneurs

In addition to investing in social entrepreneurs so that they can replicate or extend successful programs, the foundation also connects social entrepreneurs with key individuals and resources through various channels—academic, business, and community—not only to advance the efforts of individuals but also the field of social entrepreneurship. Its connectivity effort consists of endowing a center for social entrepreneurship, convening the annual Skoll World Forum on Social Entrepreneurship, and maintaining the Social Edge, an online forum for and about social entrepreneurs.

In 2003, the Skoll Foundation endowed a center at Oxford University's Said Business School to further the academic study of and nurture social entrepreneurship.[37] Its $7.5 million, five-year grant created the Skoll Centre for Social Entrepreneurship and enabled the business school to integrate social entrepreneurship into its curriculum. As the world's first program of its kind, Skoll sought to create a center designed to bring together research and teaching on social entrepreneurship. By enabling the business school to offer a one-year MBA program in social entrepreneurship, the grant provides those interested in this endeavor with the academic tools they need to go ahead and pursue their mission in life. Also, the center funds Skoll Scholars for Oxford's one-year MBA program and supports Skoll Fellows who do research in and teach social entrepreneurship.

The center also convenes the annual Skoll World Forum on Social Entrepreneurship. This forum brings together the world's leading practitioners and thinkers in the field of social entrepreneurship. Others invested in promoting the "social good" can network and learn from the preeminent exponents of new ideas and techniques to address major social problems.

Skoll and Filmanthropy

After achieving financial independence, it dawned on Skoll that he "had the opportunity to do more than write about the problems of the world."[38] With his privilege came the responsibility to give back. He realized he could "actually hire writers to write these stories about the problems of this small interconnected world. Then another light bulb went off and I realized, better than just writing stories, get them out to people in a big way, through movies, which was something nobody was doing, so in January 2004 I started Participant Productions."[39]

One of Skoll's philanthropic endeavors became making films with a social mission. He realized the media, particularly movies, offer a good way to reach people.[40] Thus, he set out to straddle the line between business and philanthropy, making "socially redeeming" movies that are "commercially viable," according to Skoll, "because I believe that movies and documentaries can be a wonderful pathway to change the world."[41]

Skoll's involvement in the motion pictures went back to 2001. Shortly after leaving eBay, he attended a small dinner party hosted by venture capitalist George Zachary. Skoll sat next to Richard Barton Lewis, a film producer whose credits included "Robin Hood: Prince of Thieves." Thereafter, as the sole investor, he put $3 million into Ovation Entertainment, Lewis's startup production company. Skoll hoped the firm would produce documentaries about social entrepreneurs that would educate the public about their activities. He spent another $4 million to save Ovation's best-known film project, "House of D," which was released in 2005. The film tanked at the box office and was universally panned by critics. Skoll had previously ended his involvement with Ovation in mid-2003.[42]

Once burned, but now more focused and savvy about the film industry, in 2004 he moved from Silicon Valley to Los Angeles. He holed up with Peter Schlessel, a former head of Columbia Pictures, and a young studio staffer, trying to figure out what a world-changing film would look like.

He established himself in Hollywood, where Participant Productions made good on its promise to produce films that are commercially and socially productive. With filmanthropy as his goal, according to Skoll, "The reason for starting this company was to leverage the power of storytelling to focus on issues that are relevant to our times. If it ends up existing in a grey market between commerciality and non-profit," it will still be worth the effort.[43]

In founding Participant Productions, Skoll sought to achieve a social impact mission through the screen, straddling business and philanthropy. Staking the "pro-social" commercial operation with $100 million for its first three years, Skoll stated, "Ultimately, the goal here is to build a brand around social relevance in the media."[44] He explained, "For us, a project that is commercially successful but doesn't [have a social impact] is a failure."[45]

With his motion picture company, Skoll hoped to inform and educate people about some of the world's bigger issues, to inspire hope and then action. For Skoll, "Time and time again, you see this outpouring from people once they're made aware they can do something. That's the principle that drives this company."[46]

Participant Productions evaluates each script equally on its creative and commercial potential and its ability to boost public awareness in one of six areas: environment; health; human rights; institutional responsibility; peace and tolerance; social and economic equity. The firm follows a three-step review process: First, the creative team looks at it; then, finance; finally, it undergoes a social review. The firm asks: does it have a "valid" social or political message and are there nonprofit, corporate and media partners that will help audiences get involved? Participant executives with nonprofit backgrounds reach out to social activist organizations with an agenda, such as the American Civil Liberties Union and the Sierra Club, and ascertain whether they can build an effective action campaign around a film. With the film venture bridging business and philanthropy, Skoll noted, "The movie helps the non-profits; the non-profits help the movie."[47]

Skepticism abounded regarding Skoll's cinema venture. Hollywood is littered with an endless stream of would-be producers. Skoll's politically-engaged movies proved them wrong. Participant Productions, as a co-financer, carved out a niche, cashing in on the politicization of American culture, the widespread anti-Bush, anti-war, anti-capitalism sentiment, led by Michael Moore's "Fahrenheit 9/11." Offering compelling, message-oriented dramas that would move public opinion and help promote social change, in 2005 the firm released its first four films, beginning with "Good Night, and Good Luck" about McCarthyism and the value of a free press. An oil espionage thriller, "Syriana," set in the context of a CIA agent frustrated by bureaucracy in his efforts to combat global injustice, took on the global oil industry and America's dependence on Middle East petroleum. "Murderball" dealt with living with a disability. Although "North Country," a film about sexual harassment, proved a box office dud, it helped ensure the renewal of the Federal Violence Against Women Act.

In 2006, Skoll followed up with the release of former Vice President Albert (Al) Gore, Jr.'s "An Inconvenient Truth," history's third highest grossing documentary (behind "Fahrenheit 9/11" and "March of the Penguins"), which generated public interest in global warming. Gore's movie won an Oscar in 2007 for the Best Documentary Film. Then came "Fast Food Nation," an exposé of the fast-food industry, released in 2006, and "Charlie Wilson's War" and "The Kite Runner," in 2007.

In funding films that bring non-frequent movie goers to theaters and serve as a vehicle for social change, Participant Productions provides an infrastructure that allows its films to make a difference far beyond the movie theater. Skoll hopes that moviegoers will participate in an issue raised by a film after viewing the cinema. He stated, "To take these movies and use them as a catalyst to actually change society, working with organizations that could be involved in these issues. Instead of people seeing a film and saying, 'I'm going to go and have a beer' they'd go, 'Wow. What can I do to help?' And I wanted to give them tools that could actually help."[48]

In an effort to make a more significant public impact, each film has a social issues campaign built around it. Skoll's company created partnerships with activist groups and organized web awareness campaigns tied to its movies. A partner social-networking website, *participant.net*, provides viewers with a way to get involved. Campaigns for its movie are rolled out on this website with the release of each film, people who are moved by a film can do something about a "cause" in real life, without giving up their lives.[49] Individuals become involved, for example, in group blogs with a topic's high profile experts. Furthermore, its larger purpose, perhaps, is to compel the media to get back to reporting in the "public interest," at least as Skoll saw it.

Reflecting on both eBay and his film production company, Skoll stated, "The heart of eBay, what made it so successful, wasn't so much the buying and the selling, which was its economic side, but the facilitation of these relationships in its public forums and question-and-answer areas. I think these days, people want to join with other people to make change. It's about leverage."[50]

Beyond the role played by social activist groups and the creative use of the web to facilitate serious conversations about issues raised in a film and to drum up support for campaigns in niche areas, Participant found and worked with the right partners. Major studios, such as Warner Bros. Entertainment (a division of Time Warner) and Paramount (part of Viacom), became co-production companies, sharing costs as well as the development and distribution functions on nearly all of Participant's films. Skoll also worked with Mark Cuban, a fellow tech billionaire and multifaceted media magnate, who owns production companies, distributors, and the Landmark theater chain, among other business ventures.

As Skoll reflected on his two and a half years of active involvement, "For me, the premise was to create a media company in the public benefit. . . . Yet I thought there was a higher leverage to come in and create movies and TV shows that were actually able to do some good in the world. Whether they make money or not is not my biggest concern. I hope they do. It shows they're commercially viable and the model is sustainable and people are seeing them. But at the end of the day, social good is our primary metric."[51] Vowing to plow any profits back into making more movies, Skoll measures each film's social action returns, so that he views even money-losing films as successful.[52]

Skoll got into movies in January 2004, when serious was hot. He found (or had brought to him) socially relevant scripts that appealed to leading stars, such as George Clooney, restive at working on forgettable, lowbrow fare. He realized that his movies could draw viewers and serve as a launching pad for grassroots activism campaigns reminiscent of the 1960s and 1970s.

Then in August 2006, Skoll stepped down as CEO of Participant Productions, but retained his role as chairman, hoping to guide the company's expansion into other media forms, such as television, and new avenues for activism. He sees Participant eventually as a "full-scale media company."[53]

As a Canadian citizen, Skoll denies that his aims are partisan, even though he tapped into the rabid anti-Bush sentiment in the middle of the first decade of the twenty-first century. According to Skoll:

> My views tend to be centrist. I'm not a big fan of George W., but my politics tend to be more Republican than not. But it depends. It goes back to when I was a kid looking at these big trends around the world. And these are really bad problems. And if people don't get involved, they are going to get worse. The reason this company [Participant Productions] exists is to bring these problems to people's attention and get them to figure out what the solution is.
>
> We don't have the answers. I don't think the Democrats have the answers and I don't think the Republicans have the answers, but together by having these things brought to public attention, we can find the answers. I believe people are basically good, and when they see a problem they'll want to solve it.[54]

Skoll sought to use movies to promote social activism, whether the suspicion of oil companies or the threat posed by global warming. A proponent of a bottom line beyond profit maximization, he stated, "To me, we're straddling the line between business and philanthropy. If a film is successful, but does no good in the world, I would consider it a failure. Whereas if a movie does some good but doesn't make a lot of money, I'd still say it was worthwhile."[55]

What is unclear is how any film will make the world a better place. How do you measure a movie's social impact, its social benefit? Is it sufficient to look to the feedback received by activist organizations, website metrics, and anecdotal reports? Do the already converted come to Skoll's movies? Is he preaching to the choir? Hard data may never be able to answer these questions.

Skoll's activities through his foundation and his film production company represent two methods of achieving the same goal. Skoll is interested in alleviating major problems he sees in the world, such as poverty and environmental degradation, through social action. On the foundation side, rather than simply donating money to nonprofits that adhere to objectives he favors, Skoll is more interested in how entities seek to achieve these goals. He looks for groups whose entrepreneurial approach allows them to achieve big tasks with comparatively small investments. Through Participant Productions, Skoll is hoping for a similar result by investing in movies he feels can change a culture's social consciousness. For Skoll, if successful, these movies will propel audiences to take action to fight social injustice, all for the price of producing a movie. The goals on both the foundation side and the film side of his philanthropy are ambitious, many would even say unrealistic and naïve, but this is exactly how Skoll felt about eBay before joining with Omidyar. In any event, Skoll led people to start looking at media, particularly movies, to achieve their philanthropic and social mission goals.

Notes

1. Luisa Kroll with Matthew Miller, "Billionaires Rankings: Index," *Forbes* 181:6 (March 24, 2008): 146-160, at 157.
2. The quotations are from Anya Kamenetz, "Moving Pictures," *Fast Company* 108 (September 2006): 90-95, at 95. For background on The Gandhi Project, see Skoll Foundation, "The Gandhi Project" <*http://www.skollfund.org/gandhi*> (April 10, 2007).
3. Douglas McGray, "Network Philanthropy," *West* (*Los Angeles Times Magazine*) January 21, 2007, 14-17, 31-32, at 31.
4. Gordon Pitts, "eBay Billionaire Aids Social Change," *Globe and Mail* (Canada), February 17, 2003, B3.
5. Rick Spence, "The Education of Jeff Skoll," *Profit* 22:6 (December 2003): 13.
6. Jeffrey Skoll, interview by Michelle Conlin, "Why Delay? Give It Away," *BusinessWeek* 3860 (December 1, 2003): 84.
7. Christopher Shulgan, "Mr. Skoll Goes to Hollywood," *Globe and Mail* (Canada), February 24, 2006, 28.
8. Skoll, interview by Conlin, "Why Delay? Give It Away."
9. For background on Omidyar and Skoll, I have drawn on Adam Cohen, *The Perfect Store: Inside Ebay* (Boston: Little, Brown, 2002): 31-33.
10. Pierre Omidyar, "The Idea Man," *Time International* 161:3 (January 27, 2003): 48.
11. Cohen, *Perfect Store*, 31.
12. Jeffrey Skoll, interview by Des Dearlove, "eBay's Jeff Skoll on Business' Social Revolution," *New Zealand Management* 51:3 (April 2004): 34-36, at 35.

13. Patrick Goldstein, "Merging Movies and Activism," *Los Angeles Times*, November 15, 2005, E1. See also Stephanie Strom, "What's Wrong With Profit?," *New York Times*, November 13, 2006, F1.
14. Skoll, interview by Dearlove, "eBay's Jeff Skoll," 35.
15. *Ibid.*, 35.
16. Alison Benjamin, "Business with a Conscience," *The Guardian* (London), November 4, 2003, 4.
17. Pitts, "eBay Billionaire." See also Jeff Skoll, interviewed by Luba Krekhovetsky, *Canadian Business* 76:2 (February 3, 2003): 54-56, at 54.
18. Beyond the scope of this book, the Pension Protection Act of 2006, Public Law 107-204, significantly increased the federal regulation of supporting organizations.
19. Sally Osberg, "Starting Skoll," September 12, 2001 <http://www.skollfoundation.org/media/published_works/sosberg/091201.asp> (September 9, 2007).
20. McGray, "Network Philanthropy," 17.
21. Skoll Foundation, "About the Skoll Foundation" <http://www.skollfund.org/aboutskoll> (April 10, 2007) and "Mission and Vision" <http://www.skollfund.org/aboutskoll/mission_vision.asp> (April 10, 2007).
22. Stephen G. Greene, "Selling Social Change," *Chronicle of Philanthropy* 16:4 (November 27, 2003): 7-9, at 8.
23. Skoll, interview by Dearlove, "eBay's Jeff Skoll," 35-36. See also Skoll Foundation, "What is a Social Enterpreneur?" <http://www.skollfund.org/aboutsocialentrepreneurship/whatis.asp> (April 10, 2007).
24. See generally David Bornstein, *How to Change the World: Social Entrepreneurs and the Power of New Ideas* (New York: Oxford, 2004) and Roger L. Martin and Sally Osberg, "Social Entrepreneurship: The Case for Definition," *Stanford Social Innovation Review* 5:2 (Spring 2007): 28-39; Nicholas D. Kristof, "Do-Gooders With Spreadsheets," *New York Times*, January 30, 2007, A23; Nicholas D. Kristof, "The Age of Ambition," *New York Times*, January 27, 2008, Week in Review Section, 18.
25. Skoll interview by Dearlove, "eBay's Jeff Skoll," 36. See also Skoll Foundation, "Mission and Vision."
26. Skoll, interview by Dearlove, "eBay's Jeff Skoll," 36. See also Bornstein, *How to Change the World*, 117-125, 200-208, 233-241.
27. Skoll Foundation, "About the Skoll Foundation."
28. Todd Cohen, "Rockefeller Foundation Launches Acumen Fund," *Non-Profit Times* 15:16 (August 15, 2001): 18.
29. Acumen Fund, "About Us" <http://www.acumenfund.org/About/> (September 13, 2007) and "Our Work" <http://www.acumenfund.org/Work/> (September 13, 2007). See also Jessi Hempel, "How Venture Philanthropists Use Design Thinking To Help Solve Real-World Problems," *BusinessWeek* 4025 (March 12, 2007): 9-12; Social World Economic Forum, "Blended Value Investing: Capital Opportunities for Social and Environmental Impact," March 2006, 57; Jennifer 8. Lee, "A Charity With an Unusual Interest in the Bottom Line," *New York Times*, November 13, 2006, F13; Jessie Hemple, "Acumen's New Model for Third-World Aid," *BusinessWeek Online*, November 10, 2006; Daniel Gross, "Fighting Poverty With $2-a-Day Jobs," *New York Times*, July 16, 2006, Section 3, 4.
30. Skoll Foundation, Press Release, "Skoll Foundation Launches $1.5 Million Partnership with Venture Philanthropy Acumen Fund," December 12, 2006.

Jeffrey Skoll and His Philanthropic Endeavors   83

31. Institute for OneWorld Health, "About Us" <http://www.oneworldhealth.org/about> (April 16, 2007), "Business Model" <http://www.oneworldhealth.org/business/index.php> (September 9, 2007), "Global Health" <http://www.oneworldhealth.org/global/index.php> (September 9, 2007), "Disease & Programs" <http://www.oneworldhealth.org/diseases/pipeline.php> (September 9, 2007). See also Trang Ho, "Victoria Hale's Medical Victory," *Investor's Business Daily*, August 14, 2007, A3; Warren Ross, "Conscientious Objectives," *Medical Marketing & Media* 42:5 (May 1, 2007): 53-58; Eric Nee, "Victoria Hall," *Stanford Social Innovation Review* 5:1 (Winter 2007): 21-23; Victoria G. Hall, "In Pursuit of the Cure," *New York Times*, December 31, 2006, Section 3, 9; Stephanie Strom, "A Small Charity Takes the Reins In Fighting a Neglected Disease, *New York Times*, July 31, 2006, A1; Jule Klotter, "Institute for OneWorld Health," *Townsend Letter for Doctors and Patients* 276 (July 1, 2006): 36; Erika Check, "Quest for the cure," *Foreign Policy* 155 (July 1, 2006): 28-36, at 35-36; Andrew Jack, "Small groups are a solution," *Financial Times* (London), October 19, 2005, 4; Victoria Hale, "Private-Sector Mercy," *New York Times*, August 19, 2005, A19; Geoffrey Cowley, "Chasing Black Fever," *Newsweek* 145:26A (June 10, 2005): 60-64; Victoria Hale, "Creating More Paths to Hope," *Newsweek* 144:23 (December 6, 2004): 80; Linda Marsa, "A World of Difference," *Los Angeles Times*, October 25, 2004, F3; Michael Bond, "Cures before Cash," *New Scientist* 183:2466 (September 25, 2004): 42-45; David Perlman, "Drug Firm Seeks Cures over Cash," *San Francisco Chronicle*, August 19, 2002, A1.

32. Skoll Foundation, Press Release, "Skoll Foundation Awards $9.5 Million To Nonprofits Around The World In Support Of Social Entrepreneurship," March 17, 2005; Institute for OneWorld Health, Press Release, "Institute for OneWorld Health Awarded Skoll Foundation's Social Entrepreneurship Award," March 21, 2005; and Skoll Foundation, "Recipients of 2005 Skoll Awards for Social Entrepreneurship" <http://www.skollfoundation.org/grantees/socialtrepreneuship/index.asp> (September 13, 2007). See also *Drug Week*, Pharmaceutical company receives Skoll award for Social Entrepreneurship," April 15, 2005, 324. The grants totaling more than $100 million by the Gates Foundation are summarized in the Institute for OneWorld Health, "History" <http://www.oneworldhealth.org/about/history.php> (September 16, 2007), notably a $46 million grant in 2006 for the development of a novel treatment for childhood diarrhea. Institute for OneWorld Health, Press Release, "Institute for OneWorld Health Awarded $46 Million Grant," November 1, 2006. See also Carl T. Hall, "Big Grant For NonProfit To Seek Diarrhea Drug for Developing World," *San Francisco Chronicle*, November 1, 2006.

33. Benetech, "About Benetech" <http://www.benetech.org/about> (April 18, 2007), "Business Model" <http://www.benetech.org/about/business_model.shtml> (April 18, 2007), "Human Rights" <http://www.benetech.org/human_rights/> (April 18, 2007), "Literacy" <http://www.benetech.org/ literary> (April 18, 2007); Jim Fruchterman, "Technology Benefitting Humanity," *Ubiquity* 5:5 (March 31-April 6, 2004) <http://www.acm.org/ubiquity/views/v5i5 ___fruchterman.htm> (April 30, 2007). See also Trang Ho, "Ratcheting Up Enterprises With A Social Vision," *Investor's Business Daily*, September 4, 2007, A10; McGray, "Men behind ebay," 17; Carrie Kirby, "Placing People before Profits," *San Francisco Chronicle*, April 14, 2003, E1; Christine Frey, "Blind Gain New Site for Literature," *Los Angeles Times*, February 25, 2002, Part 3, 6; Janet Kornblum, "Bookshare.org Opens up Choices for Disabled Readers," *USA Today*, February 21, 2002, 13B.

34. Skoll Foundation, Press Release, "Skoll Foundation Invests in 16 New Partnerships," July 25, 2002; Benetech, Press Release, "Benetech Receives Skoll Award

for Social Entrepreneurship," June 6, 2004; Skoll Foundation, Press Release, "Skoll Foundation Awards $16 Million to Nonprofits Around the World in Support of Social Entrepreneurship," March 14, 2006; Benetech, "President's Update," June 2006.
35. KickStart, "About KickStart" <http://kickstart.org/about> (April 6, 2007), "Our Approach" <http://kickstart.org/approach> (April 6, 2007), "The Technologies" <http://kickstart.org/tech> (April 16, 2007). See also *African News*, "Simple Agricultural Innovations Uplifting Lives of the Poor," August 15, 2007 (Lexis Nexis); Annelena Loeb, "Designing for the Very Poorest," *Wall Street Journal*, May 23, 2007, B3F; Ross Perlin, "A Moneymaking Water Pump," *Time* 167:22 (May 29, 2006): 52.
36. Skoll Foundation, Press Release, "Skoll Foundation Awards $9.5 Million," and Skoll Foundation, "Recipients of 2005 Skoll Awards."
37. Skoll Foundation, Press Release, "Skoll Foundation Funds Skoll Centre for Social Entrepreneurship at Oxford University," November 24, 2003. See also Della Bradshaw, "An impetus for social change," *Financial Times* (London), December 1, 2003, 12 and Todd Wallack, "eBay's First Employee Turns to Good Works," *San Francisco Chronicle*, November 20, 2003, B2.
38. Spence, "The Education of Jeff Skoll."
39. William Booth, "Lights, Camera, Social Action!," *Washington Post*, January 29, 2006, N1. See also Skoll: interview by Conlin, "Why Delay? Give It Away."
40. Shulgan, "Mr. Skoll goes to Hollywood." Alastair Smart, "Film Rich Philanthropists Have Found A New Way Of Saving The World," *Sunday Telegraph* (London), April 29, 2007, Section 7, 24, provides a useful overview of filmanthropy. See also Caryn Jones, "Movies With a Message And Their Money Trail," *New York Times*, December 7, 2005, E1.
41. Melba Newsome, "Movies with a Message," *Time* 166:25 (December 19, 2005): A13. See also Adam Lashinski, "eBay's First Hire Goes To The Movies," *Fortune* 151:5 (March 7, 2005): 36.
42. Shulgan, "Mr. Skoll goes to Hollywood."
43. Liam Lacey, "The Filmanthropist," *Globe and Mail* (Canada), September 20, 2005, R1.
44. Kamenetz, "Moving Pictures," 93.
45. Missy Schwartz, "A New Billionaire in Town," *Entertainment Weekly*, October 28, 2005, 26.
46. Kamenetz, "Moving Pictures," 93.
47. Gaby Wood, "Hollywood's new politics," *The Observer* (London), January 8, 2006, 4.
48. Peter Howell, "What's This? Idealism in the film biz?", *Toronto Star*, September 23, 2005, D1.
49. Goldstein, "Merging Movies and Activism."
50. Strom, "What's Wrong with Profit?"
51. Booth, "Lights, Camera, Social Action!"
52. Jessi Hempel, "Lights, Action, and Bleeding Hearts," *BusinessWeek* 3958 (November 7, 2005): 102.
53. Kamenetz, "Moving Pictures," 94.
54. Booth, "Light, Camera, Social Action!"
55. Goldstein, "Merging Movies and Activism."

6

Stephen Case: The Rise and Fall of a Business Empire, Then Entrepreneurship and Innovative Philanthropy

Years ago, when Steve Case thought about the Internet, he thought big. He thought technology would change the way people conduct their daily lives. When he put this ambition into practice he revolutionized the Internet and made it accessible to the average person. Case's company, America Online, Inc. (AOL), took the fear of technology out of the Internet, making "dot-com" and "megabyte" part of everyday usage. This feat was particularly extraordinary given the number and size of competitors AOL had to contend with—companies like direct-competitor Compuserve as well as giant Microsoft—and the seemingly continuous predictions in the 1990s of AOL's demise.

Case was unfazed by such predictions. Throughout his roller-coaster entrepreneurial ride, Case, a visionary business-builder, had (and continues to have) lofty ideals for what his projects can become. According to one AOL executive, for Case, "… AOL was not just something you did with your computer … it was something huge and something that would one day be as big and pervasive as the telephone or the television."[1]

At the height of the dot-com boom in 1999, AOL had become the leading Internet service provider, and Case, its CEO and chairman, had an estimated net worth of $1.5 billion.[2] This all changed after the January 2001 merger of AOL and Time Warner, followed by the collapse of the conglomerate's stock price. Case's net worth plummeted to $610 million in 2003 and then rose to $825 million in 2004,[3] after he had extricated himself from the AOL Time Warner debacle and began a new set of ventures. It continued to rise to $900 million in 2005; by 2007, *Forbes* placed his net worth in the billionaire category once again and by 2008, reached $1.2 billion.[4]

As developed in this chapter, Case has a track record of taking new technologies and making them into gigantic enterprises that change the way we live. Today, Case has brought his business-building acumen to both the entrepreneurial for-profit sphere and the philanthropic world. He has become a big proponent of hybrid philanthropy, namely, blending businesses with nonprofits, so as to enhance lives. He stated, "I think where the lines blur is where it's most interesting. I'm aiming for a more flexible tool box, not just looking at things through the prism of philanthropy or the prism of business but a fresh creative approach that uses the best of both."[5]

Seeing profit and purpose as going together and leading to a convergence of the private and social sectors, he further noted in words Pierre Omidyar could have expressed:

> Too many people still act as if the private sector and the social sector should operate on different axes, where one is all about money and the other about serving society. A better approach is to integrate these missions, with businesses that are "not-only-for-profit" and social service groups with their own earned income all contributing to positive, durable, significant social change.
>
> The real strength of organizations in this "sector-blending" space is that they don't just balance competing goals—they try to maximize both…. [P]urpose and profit aren't zero-sum, they're mutually reinforcing.[6]

Before Case could arrive at this approach, however, he built and lost one business empire, generating a considerable fortune along the way.

Background on Steve Case

Stephen M. Case was born in 1958 and grew up in an affluent suburb of Honolulu.[7] From kindergarten through the twelfth grade, he attended an exclusive, private school across the street from his home. He graduated from Williams College in 1980 with a degree in political science. An entrepreneur in college, he started various companies, such as one aimed at persuading parents to buy fruit baskets to send to their offspring during final exams. After college, he worked for Proctor & Gamble, as an assistant brand manager, trying to build brand names for several products. Then he got a job with Pepsi Co's Pizza Hut subsidiary, where his duties as a manager of new development included coming up with ideas for new pizza toppings.

In 1983, Steve, then 25, joined his brother, Daniel H. (Dan) Case III, at the annual International Consumer Electronics Show (ICES) in Las Vegas. Dan introduced Steve to William Von Meister, the founder of The Source, the first online service aimed at the average consumer. Previously, Von Meister had started a company called Digital Music, an early predecessor of downloadable music programs, such as Napster. In this early stage, however, record companies had enough power to stop Digital Music in its tracks. Using the bandwidth from Digital Music, Von Meister turned to video games. He entered into a relationship with Atari and developed a company, Control Video Corp., which allowed users to download and play video games over telephone lines. Von Meister publicized this firm at the ICES, and he ended up hiring Case initially as a marketing consultant and then as a full-time employee.

After Von Meister was forced out of Control Video by its creditors, the new management team reorganized the company into Quantum Computer Services Inc. (Quantum) in 1985 and began marketing its Q-Link online communications service, the predecessor of what would become America Online. For the next decade, from 1985 to 1995, Case focused on keeping the firm in business and getting people to believe that some day they would live in a more interactive world. By creating services people wanted and liked, he successfully lowered the barriers between computers and the average person.

Some of Case's business exploits during this period are legendary. In one of his notable marketing gambits, he went to Apple Computer's offices in California in late 1986 and camped out until Apple agreed to provide Q-Link services to the purchasers of its computers. The service became known as Apple Link. Case then engineered several company-saving deals for Quantum including one with Tandy Corp. (Radio Shack), which enabled users to communicate over telephone lines on PC-Link.

Apple eventually began to have second thoughts about licensing the use of its trademark in Apple Link to Quantum. Before it could act, Quantum dumped Apple in 1989 and changed the name of its service to AOL. The company officially became America Online, Inc. in 1991.

From 1991 to 1999, Case continued his meteoric rise at AOL, first as president (in 1991) and then as CEO and chairman. He presided over what appeared to be one of the great success stories of American business, beginning with the firm's initial public offering in 1992. In building AOL and promoting it as a simple online service for the masses, Case buried powerful competitors such as CompuServe, Prodigy, and GEnie. However, beneath the surface, all was not well with AOL.

By late 1996, facing stiff competition from other Internet service providers, AOL abandoned the hourly fee it had charged its customers and replaced it with a monthly flat rate. Users soon began to spend more time online, taxing AOL's network and reducing its profit margins. AOL then set its sights on getting companies to advertise on its online network. The firm intended the ads to keep revenues and profits soaring after the growth of its monthly subscriber fees began to ebb. However, by late 2000, failing dot-coms no longer could pay for the ads they had agreed to buy from AOL under long-term contracts, thereby placing in jeopardy a significant portion of AOL's ad business.[8]

In a decade, AOL had gone from a small Internet service provider to a hubris-driven goliath with lofty stock prices enabling it to take over a massive, old media company, Time Warner, in January 2001, at the peak of the tech bubble. Case consummated the merger by providing $156 billion of AOL stock. As chairman, he headed history's most powerful media empire—a company that owned Time, Fortune, Sports Illustrated, People, CNN, HBO and Warner Brothers. AOL's online service was supposed to be the growth engine for the merged company, offering new ways to market Time Warner's brands through the Internet.

However, none of the hoped-for synergies from the combination of AOL's Internet platform with Time Warner's diverse content of magazines, movies, and music came to fruition. The digital convergence of a media firm and an Internet company floundered and the deal proved to be a failure. AOL's online advertising revenues went into a deep slump; the growth of its online subscriber base ebbed. AOL's slumping performance dragged down the value of the merged company's stock. By mid-2002, a humbled AOL became a unit within a Time Warner division. The merger became one of the greatest business failures of all time.[9]

In addition, AOL's accounting irregularities dogged the merged entity. In March 2005, Time Warner settled U.S. Securities and Exchange Commission allegations of accounting violations at AOL.[10] This just after it had resolved U.S. Department of Justice criminal charges in December 2004. Total settlement costs for the federal probes came to $510 million, with Time Warner paying $360 million in fines and setting aside $150 million for a settlement fund for shareholders who lost money on Time Warner's stock. Previously, in early 2002, in a tacit admission that the deal had been overvalued, AOL Time Warner took a noncash $54 billion charge as a result of new accounting rules about goodwill. The firm also paid out several billion dollars to settle shareholder lawsuits.

After two years as chairman, under pressure from institutional and other major shareholders, Case resigned in January 2003, officially stepping down in May 2003. Later that same year, in September, Time Warner dropped AOL from its name. Case remained on Time Warner's board of directors until he resigned in October 2005.

Case: The Reborn Entrepreneur

Within days of his departure as Time Warner's chairman, Case spoke with Donn M. Davis, his former chief of staff at AOL and a longtime friend, about putting together a new venture. Learning from the AOL Time Warner fiasco, he wanted to return to his entrepreneurial roots. According to Case, "I was a better builder than manager.... When [AOL] went from being a little company on a crusade to a big company, I was less good at it. I was less effective."[11] Case further stated, "I've always been, because of the nature of AOL in its early days, an insurgent at the gates trying to have disruptive impact."[12]

Taking a controlling stake in any entity was important for Case. At AOL Time Warner, viewing himself as a strategic thinker with little influence on corporate strategy, he felt he was a chairman without any real portfolio. Thus, he vowed to buy a majority interest in any company he would invest in and put in place executives who would allow him to stay out of daily operations. Case indicated, "My new companies may fail, but at least I have control of my destiny."[13]

Case's new company, Revolution LLC, occupies most of his time now. Founded in April 2005,[14] Revolution is a private holding company that buys significant stakes in companies through four different subsidiaries: Revolution Health, Revolution Resorts, Revolution Living, and Revolution Money. To get it started, Case poured $125 million into the company, giving him an 80 percent ownership stake. He has committed a full $500 million over time, a considerable chuck of the billionaire's worth. As its mission, Revolution works to tie together the seemingly disparate companies it invests in. More specifically, it strives "to give people more choice, more control, and more convenience in the important aspects of their lives—and build significant companies in the process."[15]

Beyond empowering consumers in a new way, Case sought to disrupt industries. As he indicated, "It struck me that Revolution might be a good name because it does sort of summarize the approach we're trying to bring to bear, which is not an incremental, tweaking kind of thing, but really to take some risks and swing for the fences and to have a transformative impact on society, as well as to build significant businesses in the process."[16] As Revolution's website states, "We don't just aim for a return—we seek to make history.[17]

In seeking to create another AOL-like empire, Case recalled, "So, I said maybe…. I should keep doing that [building significant, valuable businesses]. Instead of taking some other path, maybe I should go back to the garage, if you will, and focus my time and attention on the thing I think I do well and that I love, which is building businesses. But not just building any business: if it's not a business that really touches consumers and really improves their lives, and if it's not a business that has the potential for significant potential—meaning multibillion-dollar potential—I don't want to do it."[18] "Revolution is all about consumer businesses that are in early stages of development," he indicated, "but are at a tipping point,"[19] where they can change lifestyles for the healthier and better.

Revolution Health. Healthcare, the focus of the leading Revolution subsidiary, Revolution Health Group LLC (Revolution Health Group), has been a major element in Case's life for a number of years. Soon after he became chairman of AOL Time Warner, in March 2001, his brother Dan was diagnosed with a brain tumor. Steve took an apartment in San Francisco to be near him and help guide him through the maze of available medical options. Steve and Dan endured duplicative forms and medical records, long waits for tests as well as confusion over options and the availability of new therapies.

Following his brother's death from brain cancer in June 2002, healthcare remained a concern of Case's. He saw how difficult it was for the privileged, such as Dan, to make well-informed decisions about their medical care. Seeing the field as complex, confusing, inefficient, and inconvenient, he pondered: why was everything so complicated; why were there so many forms; why was information hard so to come by?

In the first decade of the twenty-first century, healthcare reminded Case of the early years of the Internet: chaotic, disorganized, and intimidating to the average consumer. Seeking to improve the lot of customers, Case indicated, "I like building businesses that empower consumers by giving them more choice and control and convenience and have the power to have a transformative, disruptive impact on large, traditional, often-slow-moving industries."[20]

Case turned to providing consumer-friendly healthcare services, online and at the retail level. In December 2004, after hiring Ronald Klain, his longtime attorney with the California law firm of O'Melveny & Myers, to be his right-hand man and executive vice president, Case started the Revolution Health Group, a for-profit company in July 2005, to improve the healthcare field by empowering consumers. For Case, "It's about trying to make a difference."[21] Seeking to transform the delivery of healthcare in the United States by putting patients in charge, Case wanted to "put consumers back at the center of the health system, by giving them more choice, control and convenience...."[22]

Given Case's experience at AOL, his focus turned to creating an online community devoted to healthcare issues and medical insurance questions, and disseminating information from top clinics. To implement his vision, Case's firm, the Revolution Health Group, bought four companies which would become the building blocks of a new web portal to help consumers manage their care: MyDNA Media, a provider of health information and news; 1-800 Schedule, which helps patients find physicians and schedule appointments; Simo Software, Inc., a maker of software which enables users to keep track of their healthcare spending; Wondir Inc., an online forum linking users with others who may have answers to their healthcare questions.[23] It purchased a controlling interest in Extend Benefits LLC (now called Extend Health Inc.), which works with companies to provide individualized healthcare solutions for their employees and retirees, and TLContact, a company that provides the online health community CarePages.[24]

The Revolution Health Group launched its web consumer health portal, *RevolutionHealth.com*, which Case hopes will become one of the world's most useful websites, in April 2007.[25] Through its acquisition of HealthTalk, a site devoted to patients with chronic conditions, as well as its strategic partnership and its investment in SparkPeople, which offers diet ideas and exercise plans, later in 2007,[26] the Revolution Health became the nation's leading healthcare information site, surpassing rival *WebMD.com*. Access to information on its site is free and includes licensed content physician blogs, wellness tools, a personal health record (in which users enter data), and ratings for doctors and hospitals, with Revolution Health generating revenues through advertising. Revolution Health also has a membership option that gives subscribers an array of health-related services for an annual fee. Rather than dealing with complex insurance issues, finding the best local specialist, or searching for health information themselves, subscribers can contact Revolution Health with these questions and the company does the work for them. Thus, beyond providing information, premium members can receive assistance with health-related matters across the spectrum. The result is a sort of American Automobile Association-style service to help its premium subscribers with insurance claims, scheduling appointments, software to track medical expenses and insurance reimbursements, among other services.[27]

Seeking to make healthcare more consumer friendly, in addition to his online strategies, through the Revolution Health Group, Case bought a minority interest in InterFit Health (now called RediClinic LLC), the corporate parent of RediClinic, which is building low-cost healthcare clinics in retail locations throughout the United States. In betting on the RediClinic chain to be the big thing, Case's epiphany came when he took his daughter to an emergency room one Sunday for an ear infection. He recalled, "We waited four hours and they just weren't able to see us. This is crazy: a society in which everything is convenient other than what people care most about, which is taking care of their health."[28] Following his general business strategy, Case retains the option to purchase a majority share of the company.[29]

In providing the capital to support the national rollout of RediClinic, Case sees retail, walk-in health clinics as the antidote to the expense and inconvenience of conventional, full-service physicians' offices (often intolerably jammed) or the high cost of emergency rooms for routine care of the mildly ill. Patients visit the clinics, staffed by licensed nurse practitioners, who typically have advanced training, are able to write prescriptions in some states, and use referral arrangements with local physicians for cases beyond their scope. The clinics are setup in retail chain stores, often with pharmacies that can fill prescriptions. Offering convenience, including treating patients on a walk-in basis, evening and weekend hours, and short waits which eliminate the need for appointments, as well as low, posted prices for routine, non-urgent services and diagnoses, RediClinic comports with Case's vision of consumer-directed healthcare as a mass marketing opportunity to make primary medical care more consumer friendly and economical.

To help guide the Revolution Health Group, Case brought in three notable figures: former Federal National Mortgage Association (Fannie Mae) CEO Franklin D. Raines, once President William Jefferson Clinton's budget chief, who offers a strong perspective on healthcare policy; ex-Hewlett-Packard CEO Carly Fiorina, who brings marketing expertise; and former U.S. Secretary of State Colin L. Powell, who has a significant understanding of healthcare gained through his years in the

U.S. military. The three serve on the Revolution Health Group's board of directors and are also investors in the company.

In October 2007, Case, who serves as chief executive officer of the Revolution Health Group, reorganized it into four units: Revolution Health Network, an online clearinghouse for medical information; CarePages, an online community for the seriously ill and their loved ones; Extend Health, an insurance website for businesses; and RediClinic, a chain of healthcare clinics. As part of the restructuring, Case hired Tim Davenport, an experienced software executive, to serve as president of Revolution Health Network. Davenport oversaw the transition from a startup to an operating company, including cutting staff by 25 percent (from 240 to 180) in technology and programming while ramping up its advertising, sponsorship, and sales.[30]

Revolution Resorts. The second subsidiary of Revolution, Revolution Resorts, started with companies in which Case already had an interest. At a meeting with Donn Davis in 2003, Case mused about finding a better way to vacation than owning rarely used second homes. Through a web search of vacation resort businesses, he discovered Colorado-based Exclusive Resorts LLC, a destination club. He emailed the co-owners, Brad and Brent Handler, on May 23, 2003 and met them three days later in San Diego. After staying at one of the firm's property in Los Cabos, Mexico, on July 9, 2003, Case bought 50 percent of the company. Then, on November 22, 2004, he increased his ownership stake to eighty percent and installed Davis as CEO.

As the market-leader and the largest destination club, Exclusive Resorts buys high-end residences in desirable locations. It charges high-net worth members a hefty membership deposit, as well as an annual fee, for access to its luxury properties. Its members, who do not have an ownership stake, have the right to use an array of upscale homes for a limited number of days each year almost anytime they wish to visit, subject to rules on advance bookings and limitations on holiday slots. In targeting well-off people, who travel with large families (but do not like to stay in hotels) and who want the benefits and prestige of owning multiple homes (but not the accompanying burdens and responsibilities), Case indicated, "I like the fact that, like mortgages, this approach democratizes access, making great vacation homes more accessible and more affordable to more people than ever before."[31]

In August 2007, Case announced the launch of Revolution Places, a new destination resort company. As its first project, he proposed an $800 million, 650-acre luxury resort in Costa Rica. Exclusive Resorts will build thirty of the resort's 300 private homes and Miraval: Life in Balance, part of Revolution Living, discussed next, will operate a facility with 120 rooms and 60 villas. In targeting high-end, discerning buyers and travelers, Revolution Places will make environmental preservation and cultural authenticity priorities at each property it develops. In addition to environmentally friendly architecture, the resort in Costa Rica will buy power generated by renewable resources. It also plans recycling and solid-waste management programs.[32]

Revolution Living. Building on his interest in healthy living and wellness, Case established Revolution Living LLC, the third subsidiary of Revolution, in July 2005. Following his initial investment in Exclusive Resorts, in February 2004, Case turned his attention to Miraval Resort and Spa, a high-end Arizona spa resort, based on his belief that wellness and resorts will move from the province of the elite to the masses over the next two decades as aging baby boomers seek their comforts. On February 20, 2004, Case telephoned Miraval's co-owners, Bill O'Donnell and George Ruff, but the talks went nowhere. The next day they relented and sold Case 70 percent of their company, with Case assuming its $65 million debt.[33]

After Case took control of the spa resort, he renovated all of its rooms and added villas for purchase by people who wanted to live on its grounds. He also converted the existing Spa at Miraval into the Center for Life in Balance, headed by Andrew Weil, M.D., a renowned integrative medicine expert, and shifted its focus to health and wellness programs, following Dr. Weil's natural and preventative approach. The complex became Miraval, Life in Balance, which emphasizes a more balanced lifestyle. Miraval's goal is to incorporate mindfulness, that is, being conscious of what one is doing in the moment, into every aspect of its guests' lives, thereby making it a part of their everyday routine. Additionally, Miraval, under Case's guidance, will bring its integrative wellness approach to various projects in the United States and elsewhere.

Then in April 2005, Revolution acquired the Wisdom Media Group, Inc., a small television venture focused on health and wellness.[34] In July 2005, Case rebranded Wisdom, naming it, Lime—Healthy Living with a Twist.[35] Seeing Lime as a way to tap into emerging trends in both consumer behavior and the media, Case indicated, "Healthy living is a trend that is becoming more mainstream, and we can create a brand that unites a fragmented category.... [T]he [idea] of building a next-generation network was intriguing to me."[36] Case hopes the venture will give people easier and fuller access to information about healthy living, and a new perspective on what health and wellness entail. After shutting down its cable television network because of an audience shift, while continuing to offer programming on an on-demand basis to cable operators, the advertising-supported website currently features original videos focusing on nutrition, health, the environment, and related matters. The firm also seeks to build a "green" advertising network, representing established bloggers and websites to potential advertisers.

Revolution Living's interest in meeting consumer needs extends beyond a focus on health and wellness and into the world of car rentals. Through Revolution Living, Case bought a controlling interest in Flexcar in August 2005, after using one of its cars in Washington, DC.[37] Founded in 1999 as a public-private operation in Seattle, Washington, Flexcar provided short-term auto rentals in congested urban centers for consumers who want to rent a car by the hour rather than own one. With Revolution's infusion of capital in Flexcar, the company added newer cars to its fleets, increased the number of locations where its cars are available, and upgraded its technology.[38] It expanded from Seattle to eleven other cities, including Portland, Oregon, San Francisco, Los Angeles, San Diego, Washington, DC, Philadelphia, Baltimore, Pittsburgh, and Atlanta.

By enabling members to reserve cars at locations and in blocks of time that met their needs, for Case, Flexcar offered two attractions. First, it gave consumers a money saving alternative to car ownership. Second, it helped reduce pollution and urban parking congestion. Fewer cars on the street mean lower emissions and energy use. It also served those frustrated with traditional car rental agencies.

Flexcar did not achieve profitability. After buying the firm, Case noted, "We have a business plan, but I am not focused on short-term profit. We are not in a build-to-flip mode. We are in a build-to-last mode."[39] However, in 2008, Flexcar merged with its leading competitor, Zipcar, Inc., in the hope of achieving profitability within one year. Case rolled his entire stake in Flexcar into the combined company, now known as Zipcar.[40]

Revolution Money. In September 2007, Case announced a new entity, Revolution Money, an outgrowth of GratisCard Inc., a credit card company he started in 2006. Revolution Money sought to drive potentially the biggest change in credit cards since their introduction decades ago. It launched two products. The first, a type of anonymous personal identification number-protected credit card, Revolution Card, does not display an account number or a cardholder's name, thereby reducing the chances of identity theft and fraudulent charges. Cardholders apply for credit lines and load money onto the card. Amounts loaded are moved from a bank account to the card via an automated clearinghouse network. To attract merchants to the system, the card allows them to use the Internet to reduce the traditional credit card fees they pay. The second product, an online system, Revolution Money Exchange, will compete with eBay's PayPal and Google Checkout's payment services. It allows free online payments and money transfers and lets members of online social networking sites send money to one another.[41]

Case: The Innovative Philanthropist

Case started his own foundation, The Stephen Case Foundation, with his wife Jean, in 1997. In comparison to Gates and others, the Case Foundation's assets remain modest. As a result of the decline in the price of AOL Time Warner stock and continued grantmaking, the value of the foundation's assets plummeted from $145 million at the end of 1999 to $88.9 million in 2000, dropping to $83 million in 2001 and then to $42.4 million in 2002.[42] The latest data puts the Case Foundation's assets at just under $23.5 million.[43]

Case initially found it hard to give away money.[44] With many nonprofits lacking scalability and sustainability, he came to see the need for these entities to create and implement a business model focused on their being more entrepreneurial and their generating earned income, so as to reduce their reliance on grants. Similar to Skoll, he turned to existing nonprofits, with a track record that could be taken to the next level, rather than on starting new endeavors.

To help target its giving and assist its grantees to go to scale, the foundation came to focus on three strategic themes, not specific causes. To reflect its "commitment to finding lasting solutions to complex social challenges," the foundation seeks to implement three strategies: encouraging collaboration between companies and nonprofit organizations to achieve better and more long-lasting results; supporting successful leaders; and fostering entrepreneurship in the nonprofit sector.[45] The foundation strives to apply these broad strategies to: meet the needs of underserved children and families; create thriving and sustainable economic development for Third World communities; bridge cultural and religious divides; expand civic engagement and volunteerism; and accelerate innovative approaches to healthcare.

The foundation has adopted a hybrid approach to achieve its objectives. According to Ben Binswanger, the chief operating officer of the Case Foundation, "It all becomes what are your end goals and how are you going to get to them. If there are social problems that we're trying to address, maybe some of those need to be addressed in a different sphere, and maybe they can be addressed more quickly and more flexibly by employing for-profit dollars in conjunction with nonprofit dollars."[46]

Examples of the Case Foundation's Hybrid Approach

Grants to PlayPumps, MissionFish, endeavors in Hawaii, and brain cancer research as well as its online initiatives illustrate the foundation's hybrid approach. In September 2006, the Case Foundation and the United States government announced a partnership to bring more clean water to sub-Saharan Africans.[47] The project demonstrates how a foundation, a nonprofit organization, a for-profit entity, and the public sector can constructively work together as an innovative venture to solve a problem that is too big for any one sector. As part of a $16.4 million public-private initiative, with the U.S. government pledging $10 million over three years to the project, the foundation made a $5 million grant to PlayPumps International, a nonprofit organization in Johannesburg, South Africa that developed a new approach to increasing access to clean water in rural African villages.

PlayPumps installs water pumps near schools and connects them to playground merry-go-rounds. Each merry-go-round powers a pump to draw water up a pipe from a drilled well. As children play on the PlayPump system, they not only draw up clean water previously held between underground layers of rock or soil but also have fun. Once pumped, the water from the ground is held in 2,500-liter above-ground storage tanks where local families draw their water. When a tank is full, the excess water is used for irrigation.

The pump is highly effective. It can pump water up from 100 feet underground, and pumps at a maximum rate of 1,400 liters per hour, far more than a traditional hand-pump can manage. Furthermore, the system prevents local women from having to walk long distances to obtain clean water and enables girls to stay in school rather than searching for water each day. The storage tank doubles as a public service advertising machine, where Roundabout Outdoor, a for-profit advertising firm based in Johannesburg, South Africa, displays billboards giving local residents information on health concerns, such as HIV, while simultaneously generating enough revenue from the advertisements to pay for the ongoing pump maintenance.

Various public sector entities also play a role. A national government, such as South Africa, contributes to the venture by handing over the boreholes and the wells. Local governments help install the pumps. Donors, including philanthropists such as the Case Foundation, and public sector organizations, such as The World Bank, pay for the cost of a pump, which runs $14,000 to install.

The Case Foundation is experimenting with other entrepreneurial-like approaches to giving. It made a grant of $170,000 that works as an investment in MissionFish, owned and operated as a service of the nonprofit Points of Light Foundation (now known as the Points of Light Institute).[48] The name came from the MissionFish founders' belief that auction sales on eBay could help generate a steady source of revenue for charities, thereby enabling them to focus more on their missions and less on fundraising.

The idea behind MissionFish is essentially to do for nonprofits what eBay does for individuals and businesses, as discussed in Chapters 4 and 5. It handles fundraising for charities on eBay in a section of the website called Giving Works, thereby bridging the in-kind items donors want to sell with items buyers desire and the cash nonprofits wish to receive. Individuals and companies buy and sell items in an online auction. The seller then donates anywhere from 10 to 100 percent of the sale price to a nonprofit organization of his, her, or its choice that is registered with MissionFish. Serving as a clearinghouse, MissionFish vets the status of nonprofit entities, accepts payments for sellers on behalf of their designated charities, with buyers paying MissionFish a commission based on the final price of an item.[49]

As structured, the grant in the form of a social enterprise investment gives the Case Foundation the equivalent of an equity stake in the charitable auction business. Profits generated by MissionFish not only help support other Points of Light Institute programs but also provide a source of new charitable funds for the foundation.[50]

Case, a native of Hawaii, is also blending for-profit and nonprofit approaches in his home state. On the business side, in 1999, for $40 million Case bought a 41.2 percent stake in Maui Land & Pineapple Company, Inc., a for-profit company that grows and markets pineapples and develops, sells, and manages property at its Kapalua Resort.[51] Then, in November 2005, he invested another $10.2 million to bring his stake in the company to 47.1 percent.[52] The firm is increasingly involved with luxury real estate development rather than with growing pineapples. In March 2007, it announced the purchase of a 22 percent stake in the Kapalua Ritz-Carlton Resort.

Case's nonprofit involvement with Hawaii has mirrored his foundation's overarching goals of alleviating poverty, creating sustainable economic development, and increasing civic engagement. The foundation has funded the construction of numerous homes in Hawaii through its donations of $5,000,000 to Habitat for Humanity. It has made grants aggregating $750,000 to the Hawaii Community Foundation to help nonprofit leaders develop their management skills through the PONO (Promoting Outstanding Nonprofit Organizations) Leadership Program. Through a three-year, $300,000 investment, the Case Foundation helped strengthen the University of Hawaii Business Plan Competition, which allowed the introduction of a social enterprise category in the competition. For purposes of the competition, a social enterprise is a nonprofit or for-profit business venture that strives to achieve financial self-sufficiency and a quantifiable bottom line of both financial and business returns. Through the Maui Land & Pineapple, Case is also supporting other entrepreneurial development programs in Hawaii, such as the effort spearheaded by the Sustainable Living Institute of Maui, which is giving local community college students training in land-based arts with the goal of creating a new generation of agricultural entrepreneurs who will emphasize locally grown foods and preserve Maui's natural beauty.[53]

By making grants totaling $5,500,000 the Case Foundation also supports Accelerate Brain Cancer Cure, Inc. (ABC^2), a nonprofit organization, started by the Case family to promote research and to find a cure for brain cancer which resulted in the death of Case's brother, Dan.[54] To get more promising drugs more quickly into the clinical pipeline, ABC^2 has sponsored research on brain cancer therapies and fostered collaboration among researchers, pharmaceutical companies, and the federal government. It brought together experts from these three areas to share and build support for ongoing research. Case also created a venture capital fund, BrainTrust Accelerator Fund, to invest in small companies engaged in various aspects related to brain diseases, not just brain cancer, thereby assisting firms too far along for philanthropy but too immature for corporate investment. A share of the management fees and profits realized by the fund will go to ABC^2, among other brain charities.

Promoting Innovative Approaches to Giving

The foundation has sought to expand the pool of potential donors by democratizing philanthropy and making it more transparent. In 2006, it created an online guide to charitable contributions with information on giving and dozens of links to charities' websites. The goal of the guide, the brainchild of Jean Case, Case's wife, is to make the foundation's website a bridge between nonprofits working on interesting projects and people who want to become involved in efforts, such as KickStart, discussed in Chapter 5, which develops simple technologies that help turn subsistence farms into commercial enterprises. According to Jean Case, "Connection points are needed probably as much as dollars."[55]

Continuing its innovative strategy, in mid-2007, the Case Foundation launched Make It Your Own Awards. The foundation offered the public a direct role in deciding who should receive $300,000 of its grants, thereby reaching outside its own inner circle. It asked individuals and small, local nonprofit entities to send ideas for improving their communities. A group of judges then selected one hundred of the submissions and requested a more formal proposal. Another panel of judges selected twenty finalists, with each receiving $10,000. Then, the public voted online on these twenty, with the top four vote getters receiving an additional $25,000.[56]

Then in December 2007, the foundation launched America's Giving Challenge, one of the nation's most ambitious efforts to draw the grass-roots public to philanthropy through the Internet. The initiative, featured in an issue of *Parade* magazine, sought to have ordinary people go online, find a cause and give money, as little as $10, and encourage their friends and family to do the same, to charities around the globe. The foundation also introduced another challenge at Facebook, an online social networking site. Through a "Causes" application, users of Facebook could affiliate with and donate to any of 1.5 million charities. Through the initiative, the foundation awarded $750,000 to charities that vied for prizes in the online giving experiment, with prizes going to the nonprofits that attracted the greatest number of unique donors, not those that raised the most money.[57]

Hopefully, these efforts, called philanthropulism, will spur other philanthropic organizations to consider ways not only to increase access to new ideas and involve a broader range of individuals in decision making but also to encourage grass-roots giving through the Internet. As Ms.

Case stated, "We've always asked how we can leverage our resources to engage a larger population, how can we get the most Americans involved in charitable giving and action."[58]

Case's hybrid approach to business and philanthropy is emblematic of the larger shift in charity giving from old-style megafoundations that give money to noble, but often ineffective causes, to multifaceted organizations that seek both to do good and to achieve either a profit or scalability and sustainability within a nonprofit content.

Case, in particular, has taken the approach of combining philanthropy and business to a new level. His foundation combines old-style giving to philanthropic causes that seek scalability and sustainability. Furthermore, Case's company, Revolution LLC, a for-profit firm, that seeks large returns on its investments, but chooses its endeavors based on Case's ideals for human living that combine making a difference in people's lives and having a positive impact on the world. If the goals for his foundation and for-profit ventures prove successful, Case will build more than nonprofit organizations and business entities. By blending purpose and profit, he will demonstrate that entrepreneurs can do well and do good at the same time and help solve large-scale social problems.

Notes

1. Nina Munk, *Fools Rush In: Steve Case, Jerry Levin, and the Unmaking of AOL Time Warner* (New York: HarperBusiness, 2004), 71.
2. Peter Newcomb, "The Ranking," *Forbes* 164:9 (October 11, 1999): 414-418, at 416.
3. David Armstrong and Peter Newcomb, "The Forbes 400," *Forbes* 172:7 (October 6, 2003): 136-284, at 170; David Armstrong and Peter Newcomb, "The Forbes 400 Index," *Forbes* 174:7 (October 11, 2004): 270-278, at 270.
4. Luisa Kroll with Matthew Miller, "Billionaire Rankings: Index," *Forbes* 181:6 (March 24, 2008); 146-160, at 148; Luisa Kroll and Allison Fass, "The World's Billionaires: United States," *Forbes* 179:6 (March 26, 2007) 154-168, at 168; Matthew Miller and Peter Newcomb, "The Forbes 400: The Digirati," *Forbes* 176:7 (October 10, 2005): 102-110, at 110.
5. Stephanie Strom, "What's Wrong with Profit?" *New York Times*, November 13, 2006, F1.
6. Steve Case, "Purpose and Profit Go Together," *Wall Street Journal*, May 10, 2005, B2. See also Peter Karoff with Jane Maddox, *The World We Want: New Dimensions in Philanthropy and Social Change* (Lanham, MD: AltaMira, 2007), 28-35.
7. For background on Case and AOL I have drawn on Kim Issac Eisler, "Second Coming," *Washingtonian*, February 2007, 58-61, 132-134; Kara Swisher, *aol.com: How Steve Case Beat Bill Gates, Nailed the Netheads, and Made Millions in the War for the Web* (New York: Random House, 1998), 15-16, 24-28, 30, 33-34, 49-56; Munk, *Fools*, 72-84; Alex Klein, *Stealing Time: Steve Case, Jerry Levin, and the Collapse of AOL, Time Warner* (New York: Simon & Schuster, 2003), 9-63; Mark Leibovich, *The New Imperialists* (Paramus, NJ: Prentice Hall, 2002), 193-

217; Ben Steverman, "Steve Case Made Sure To Put America Online," *Investor's Business Daily*, April 18, 2007, A3; Mark Leibovich, "From Suburban Roots To a Global Ambition," *Washington Post*, June 4, 2000, A1; Marc Gunther, "The Internet is Mr. Case's Neighborhood," *Fortune* 137:6 (March 30, 1998): 68-80; Amy Cortese et al, "The Online World of Steve Case," *BusinessWeek* 3471 (April 15, 1996): 78-81.
8. Alec Klein, "Unconventional Transactions Boosted Sales," *Washington Post*, July 18, 2002, A1.
9. The collapse of AOL Time Warner is detailed in Munk, *Fools* and Klein, *Stealing Time*.
10. U.S. Securities and Exchange Commission, Release 2005-38, "SEC Charges Time Warner with Fraud, Aiding and Abetting Frauds by Others, and Violating a Prior Cease-and-Desist Order," March 21, 2005. See also David Vise, "Time Warner Settles AOL Cases For $510 Million," *Washington Post*, December 16, 2004, A1.
11. Catherine Yang, "Another Case Entirely," *BusinessWeek* 3928 (April 11, 2005): 64-68.
12. Nina Munk, "Steve Case's New Act," *New York Times*, June 19, 2005, Section 3, 5.
13. Yang, "Another Case Entirely."
14. Revolution, Press Release, "Steve Case Launches Revolution," April 4, 2005.
15. Revolution LLC (Revolution), "Revolution Is" <*http://www.revolution.com/revolutionis*> (April 20, 2007).
16. Munk, "Steve Case's New Act."
17. Revolution, "Revolution Is."
18. Munk, "Steve Case's New Act."
19. Yuki Noguchi, "Case Uses Then Invests in Car-Sharing Firm," *Washington Post*, August 31, 2005, D1.
20. Munk, "Steve Case's New Act." For the disruptive innovation model see Joseph L. Bower and Clayton M. Christensen, "Disruptive Technologies: Catching the Wave," *Harvard Business Review* 73:1 (January-February 1995): 43-53.
21. Karen Breslau, "Steve Case," *Newsweek* 145:24 (June 13, 2005): 60. See generally, David Stires and Christopher Tkaczyk, "The (R)evolution of Steve Case," *Fortune* 152:10 (November 14, 2005): 88-96; Kim Clark, "The Case for Healthcare," *U.S. News & World Report* 139:14 (October 17, 2005): 36-38; David A. Vise, "Diving In Headfirst," *Washington Post*, May 4, 2005, E1.
22. Revolution, Press Release, "World-Class Board and Investor Group Joins With Steve Case to Create Revolution Health Group, the First Comprehensive Consumer-Driven Health Care Company," July 7, 2005.
23. Revolution, Press Release, "Revolution Health Group Announces Initial Acquisitions," October 5, 2005 and Revolution Health Group, "About Revolution Health" <*http:www.revolutionhealth.com/about*> (April 17, 2007). See also Alan Murray, "Case Study," *Wall Street Journal*, October 5, 2005, A2.
24. Stacey Lawrence, "Online Health Care Next for AOL's Steve Case," *CIO-Insight*, October 6, 2005 <*http://www.cioinsight.com/print_article*> (July 19, 2007); Annys Shin, "Revolution Invests in Convenient Care," *Washington Post*, October 6, 2005, D4.
25. Revolution, Press Release, "Revolution Health Group Launches RevolutionHealth.com," April 19, 2007.
26. Revolution Health, Press Release, "Revolution Health Acquires HealthTalk," December 5, 2007 and Revolution Health, Press Release, "Revolution Health Announces Strategic Partnership, Financial Investment in SparkPeople," December 5,

2007. See also *Health & Medicine Week*, "Revolution Health Acquires HealthTalk" (December 17, 2007): 3166 and Thomas Heath, "Revolution Health Buys Stakes in Two Web Sites," *Washington Post*, December 5, 2007, D4.

27. Milt Freudenheim, "AOL Founder Hopes to Build a New Giant Among Bevy of Health Care Web Sites," *New York Times*, April 16, 2007, C1; Annys Shin, "A Big-Ticket Start-Up With a Nonprofit Vibe," *Washington Post*, February 27, 2007, D1; Christopher Lawton, "New Services Help Unsnarl Medical Bills," *Wall Street Journal*, September 4, 2007, D1.

28. Milt Freudenheim, "Attention Shoppers," *New York Times*, May 14, 2006, Section 1, 1; Jonathan Birchall, "Walk-In Clinics Get a Foot in the Door of US Health Market," *Financial Times* (London), November 2, 2005, 9; Daniel Yi, "Latest Retail Niche," *Los Angeles Times*, July 18, 2006, C1; Julie Schmidt, "Could Walk-In Retail Clinics Help Slow Rising Health Costs?," *USA Today*, August 24, 2006, 1A; *Economist*, "McClinics," 383:8524 (April 14, 2007): 78-79; Michael Johnsen, "Clinics 'Redi' for Health Care Platform Whose Time Has Come," *Drug Store News* 29:6 (April 23, 2007): 20; Erik L. Goldman, "Wal-Mart to open 2,000 RediClinics," *Family Practice News* 37:12 (June 15, 2007): 1-2; David Whelan, "Paper? Plastic? Penicillin," *Forbes* 180:12 (December 10, 2007): 74-76. For a critical assessment of drugstore clinics, especially by physicians who are not as fond of them as many consumers are, see Kim Krisberg, "Retail-Based Health Clinics Grow in Popularity Nationwide," *Nation's Health* 37:7 (September 1, 2007): 1-3; Sarah Kershaw, "Drugstore Clinics Spread, and Scrutiny Grows," *New York Times*, August 23, 2007, A1; Zachary M. Seward, "States Boost Scrutiny of Drugstore Clinics," *Wall Street Journal*, August 9, 2007, D1; Daniel McGinn and Karen Springen, "Express-Lane Medicine," *Newsweek* 150:5 (July 30, 2007): 44; Michelle Andrews, "In-Store Clinics Give Doctors Heartburn," *U.S. News & World Report* (July 20, 2007) <http://health.usnews.com/usnews/health/articles/070720/20clinics> (September 13, 2007); Laura Landro, "The Informed Patient," *Wall Street Journal*, July 26, 2006, D1.

29. Munk, "Steve Case's New Act."

30. Thomas Heath, "Case's Revolution Health to Lay Off 60 Workers in Restructuring," *Washington Post*, October 24, 2007, D4. Revolution Health implemented more layoffs in 2008. Thomas Heath, "Revolution Health to Lay Off 50 Employees," *Washington Post*, June 7, 2008, D2.

31. Ray A. Smith, "Time-Shares for the Jet Set," *Wall Street Journal*, December 3, 2003, B1. See also Shelley Emling, "AOL founder intrigued by vacation club," Atlanta Journal-Constitution, June 26, 2005, 3C; Daniel McGinn, "Man of Leisure," *Newsweek* (Business Plus) 148:14 (October 2, 2006): E8-E16; Yang, "Another Case Entirely."

32. Lillian Ross, "Spa Man," *New Yorker* 83:19 (July 9, 2007): 38; *Washington Post*, "Steve Case Puts His Money into the Balanced Life," November 7, 2005, D2; Teya Vitu, "Just Don't Call It a Spa," *Tucson Citizen*, December 5, 2005, 1D.

33. Revolution, Press Release, "Revolution Launches New Luxury Resort Development Company," August 3, 2007. See also Kendra Marr, "Steve Case's Eco Getaway," *Washington Post*, August 3, 2007, D1; "AOL Founder Turns to Eco-Resorts," *New York Times*, August 19, 2007, K2; Lisa Chamberlain, "Luxury Lodging for the Eco-Tourist," *New York Times*, November 25, 2005, Sunday Business Section, 21.

34. "Steve Case's Revolution Continues to Build Portfolio in the Wellness Sector with Acquisition of Wisdom Media Group's Assets," April 5, 2005 <http://www.lime.com/node/3104> (February 24, 2008).

35. "Steve Case's Revolution Living Unveils Bold New Name, Logo and Rebranding for Fall Launch of Wisdom Media" <http://www.lime.com/node/3102> (February 24, 2008).
36. Saul Hansell, "Tapping a New Age on the Web, Cellphone and TV," *New York Times*, November 21, 2005, C6.
37. Revolution, Press Release, "Steve Case's Revolution Acquires Flexcar," August 31, 2005.
38. For background on the start-up of Flexcar, see Kortney Stringer, "How Do You Change Consumer Behavior?", *Wall Street Journal*, March 17, 2003, R6. See also Annys Shin, "Flexcar Receives Infusion Of Cash," *Washington Post*, June 30, 2006, D1 and Jim Hopkins, "Tired of Costs, Hassles, some City Dwellers Turn to Car-Sharing," *USA Today*, September 15, 2005, 4B.
39. Vikas Bajaj, "A Few Keyboard Clicks Put Car Sharers on Wheels," *New York Times*, November 30, 2005, C1. See also Mike Beirne, "Temporary Plates," *Brandweek* 48:27 (July 9, 2007): 30-34.
40. Revolution, Press Release, "Zipcar and Flexcar Agree To Merge," October 31, 2007. See also Thomas Heath, "Car-Sharing Leaders Expect to Turn Profit Within a Year," *Washington Post*, October 31, 2007, D1; Dominic Gates, "Car-Sharing Firms Join Forces," *Seattle Times*, October 31, 2007, E1; Darren Everson, "Car-Sharing Firms to Merge," *Wall Street Journal*, November 1, 2007, D3.
41. Revolution LLC, Press Release, "Revolution Joined by Industry Legends and Major Banks to Launch Revolutionary Payment System," September 24, 2007. See also Jefferson Graham, "Talkin' about a Revolution in Transferring Money Online," *USA Today*, November 7, 2007, 3B; Richard Mullins, "Wikipedia Lost; Revolution Won," *Tampa Tribune*, September 26, 2007, Business Section, 1; Thomas Heath, "Case Launches Online Credit Card Company," *Washington Post*, September 25, 2007, D4; Leslie Cauley, "Account Number, named not on card," *USA Today*, September 24, 2007, 1B.
42. Jacqueline L. Salmon, "Souring Economy Spells Tough Times for Charities," *Washington Post*, November 21, 2002, B6 and Jacqueline L. Salmon, "Rising Grants Not Hitting Home," *Washington Post*, December 8, 2003, B1.
43. The Stephen Case Foundation, Internal Revenue Service Form 990-PF, 2005 (Case Foundation, 2005 Form 990-PF).
44. Steve Case and Jane Wales Public Conversation, 2005 Slate 60 Conference.
45. Case Foundation, "About Us" <http://www.casefoundation.org/about/overview> (April 19, 2007).
46. Nicole Wallace, "Blending Business and Charity," *Chronicle of Philanthropy* 18:24 (September 28, 2006): 14-15, at 15. Four foundations, including The Case Foundation and The Bill & Melinda Gates Foundation, are collaborating with MTV, in testing a social networking website, *ThinkMTV.com*, intended to encourage activism among young people. Stephanie Strom, "Charities Tie to MTV Angers Nonprofits," *New York Times*, September 27, 2007, A20.
47. U.S. Agency for International Development, Fact Sheet, "U.S. Launches Public-Private Partnership for Clean Water in Africa," September 20, 2006; Mrs. Laura Bush, First Lady, "Mrs. Bush's Remarks at Clinton Global Initiative Annual Meeting," September 20, 2006; Case Foundation, "Case Foundation, U.S. Government Partner to Bring Clean Water to Africa," September 20, 2006 <http://casefoundation.org/web> (July 24, 2007); Case Foundation, "Play Pumps" <http://www.casefoundation.org/partners/playpumps> (April 9, 2007). See also Wallace, "Blending Business and Charity," 15 and Strom, "What's Wrong With Profit?"

48. The Stephen Case Foundation, Internal Revenue Service Form 990-PF, 2004 (Case Foundation, 2004 Form 990-PF), Part XV-Grants and Contributions Paid During The Year.
49. MissionFish, "About Us" <http://www.missionfish.org/About/about.jsp> (April 6, 2007); Case Foundation, "MissionFish" <http://www.casefoundation.org/partners/missionfish> (April 9, 2007). See also Jacqueline Trescott, "With Ebay Auctions, Theaters Bid On a New Brand of Fund Raising," *Washington Post*, December 28, 2004, C1; Ralph Frammolino, "Ebay to Add Feature to Certify Charity Sales," *Los Angeles Times*, September 1, 2003, C2; Clint Carpenter and Jeff Berger, "Innovative Fund Raising Ideas Bring In Cash For Bold Organizations," *NonProfit Times* 7:15 (April 1, 2001): 32-34; Nicole Wallace, "Ebay Will Donate Some Auction Fees," *Chronicle of Philanthropy* 17:11 (March 17, 2005): 32.
50. Wallace, "Blending Business and Charity," 15.
51. Hoover's In-Depth Company Records, Maui Land & Pineapple Co., Inc., April 4, 2007.
52. *Honolulu Star-Bulletin*, "Case Raises Stake in Maui Land & Pineapple Co.," November 19, 2005 <http://starbulletin.com/print/2005.php?fr=/2005/11/19/business/story> (September 24, 2007).
53. The Stephen Case Foundation, Internal Revenue Service Form 990-PF, 2000, Part XV - Grants and Contributions Paid During The Year; The Stephen Case Foundation, Internal Revenue Service Form 990-PF, 2002 (Case Foundation, 2002 Form 990-PF), Part XV–Grants and Contributions Paid During The Year; The Stephen Case Foundation, Internal Revenue Service Form 990-PF 2003 (Case Foundation, 2003 Form 990-PF), Part XV–Grants and Contributions Paid During The Year; Case Foundation, 2004 Form 990-PF, Part XV–Grants and Contributions Paid During The Year; Case Foundation, 2005 Form 990-PF, Part XV–Grants and Contributions Paid During The Year; Case Foundation, "Investing in Hawaii's Future" <http://www.casefoundation.org/partners/hawaiifuture> (April 9, 2007); University of Hawaii at Manoa, College of Business, Press Release, "Case Foundation to Sponsor UH Business Plan Competitions," February 7, 2005.
54. Case Foundation, 2002 Form 990-PF, Part XV–Grants and Contributions Paid During The Year; Case Foundation, 2003 Form 990-PF, Part XV–Grants and Contributions Paid During The Year; Case Foundation, 2004 Form 990-PF, Part XV–Grants and Contributions Paid During The Year; The Case Foundation, "ABC²" <http://www.casefoundation.org /partners/abc> (April 9, 2007) and Acclerated Brain Cancer Cure, "About Us" <http://www.abc2.org> (April 6, 2007). See also Karoff with Maddox, *The World We Want*, 30-32.
55. Stephanie Strom, "Web Site Promotes a Holiday Gift Idea," *New York Times*, December 20, 2006, A24.
56. "Case Foundation Launches Make It Your Own Awards" <http://www.casefoundation.org/make-it-your-own> (February 24, 2008) and "Case Foundation Names Top 100 Ideas for Make It Your Own Awards" <http://www.casefoundation.org/make-it-your-own> (February 24, 2008). See also Stephanie Strom, "Foundation Lets Public Award Money," *New York Times*, June 26, 2007, A13.
57. Case Foundation, "The 2007 Giving Challenge" <http://giving.casefoundation.org/givingchallenge> (February 24, 2008). See also Katherine Shaver, "Two Contests Spur Online Giving," *Washington Post*, February 21, 2008, Metro Section, B3; Stephanie Strom, "Charities Vie for Prizes in Online Giving Experiment," *New York Times*, January 31, 2008, A19; Stephanie Strom, "Foundation Testing Potential Of Philanthropy via Internet," *New York Times*, December 13, 2007, A32; Philip Rucker, "Twin Efforts Aim to Popularize Online Giving," *Washington Post*, December 13, 2007, A11.
58. Strom, "Foundation Testing Potential."

7

Sergey Brin, Larry Page, and Google.org: The Corporation as Philanthropist

In the year 2000, as dot-coms were starting to succumb to the bursting tech bubble, the general public began hearing of a search engine called Google. The company's search engine was able to obtain faster, more accurate results than any other search engine.

Google Inc. had been around as a privately-held corporation since 1998, but in the beginning it remained a search engine that appealed to a select group that formed a Google cult. It was not until 2000 that the firm attained enough popularity that it could start selling and profiting from advertisements. Mainly through word-of-mouth, Google's popularity skyrocketed until it became, by far, the most popular search engine on the Internet.

Google Inc., whose annual revenues exceeded $16 billion in 2007, trumpets itself as an unconventional corporation.[1] As such, it wants to build a different model of philanthropy. According to Sheryl Sandberg, then a Google vice president, a board member of *Google.org*, the firm's philanthropic arm, and apparently the unseen force behind the unit's creation, "We are looking at the most efficient and effective ways to solve the world's largest problems."[2]

Sergey Brin and Larry Page, as the co-founders of Google and its controlling shareholders, set up a hybrid nonprofit-for-profit fund to be used for solving societal problems. Unlike Pierre Omidyar's hybrid vehicle, discussed in Chapter 4, Google's fund is held within the corporation. The hybrid fund, *Google.org*, combines the work of the Google Foundation, a nonprofit 501(c)(3) organization, formed by Google Inc. with a $90 million endowment, together with a for-profit arm funded by a contribution of a large number of the firm's shares and a specified allocation of the corporation's profits. *Google.org* serves as the focus for the corporation's philanthropic endeavors. Along with the Omidyar

Network, it is among the leading donors experimenting with the non-profit–for profit model.

As the co-founders of Google, by early 2007 Brin and Page each had an estimated net worth of $16.6 billion, ranking number 26 on *Forbes'* list of the world's billionaires.[3] With surge in the value of Google stock, by March 2008 *Forbes* placed the net worth of Brin at $18.7 billion and Page at $18.6 billion.[4] Although their personal plans for charitable giving are not public, theirs is an amazing American success story of two unlikely billionaires.

Background on Sergey Brin and Larry Page

Sergey Brin and Larry Page took very different paths to their meeting place as fellow Ph.D. students in computer science at Stanford University.[5] When Brin was six, his family fled Russian anti-Semitism and settled in suburban Maryland, outside of Washington, DC. Sergey attended public school and quickly set himself apart from his peers. He enrolled at the University of Maryland while still in high school and received his undergraduate degree with high honors at age nineteen. His accomplishments were distinguished enough to qualify him for a National Science Foundation graduate fellowship, which enabled him to attend Stanford University for graduate school.

Page, born in Michigan, was also an unusually intelligent child. As the son of a computer science professor, he was exposed early and often to the newest technology, and was fascinated by it. "One of the early things I remember Larry was typing *Frog and Toad Together* into his computer, one word at a time, when he was six years old," recalled Page's older brother, Carl, Jr.[6] Later, when Page was in high school in East Lansing, he built a working printer out of Legos. After high school, Larry followed family tradition by enrolling at the University of Michigan, graduating in 1995. In March 1995, Larry met Sergey on a tour that the university arranged for prospective computer science graduate students. Brin, who acted as the tour guide for the group, had already spent one year in the graduate program.

Brin and Page quickly connected and began spending long nights in Page's office talking about the potential of the Internet. Their enthusiasm found focus as Page examined early search engines, such as AltaVista and Lycos, and discovered that these tools simply matched the words in a search to those found on web pages, thereby yielding largely random results. Page and Brin started tossing around the idea that a search engine would work better if it prioritized its results based primarily on the number of web pages that linked to a particular result. Similar to the number of times a scholarly work is cited by others, Page and Brin realized that a website was more likely to be respected if many other sites linked to it. With users determining which websites were the best, popularity became the key.

Recognizing that they may have just hit on a big idea, the two dropped out of Stanford and launched Google in 1998, which quickly became the Internet's most prominent search engine company. ("Google" is a play on the mathematical term, Google, the number designed by one followed by one hundred zeros.) To get the company up and running, they initially obtained financing from the Stanford University endowment and two "angel" investors. They raised another $25 million from two leading venture capital firms, Kleiner Perkins Caufield & Byers and Sequoia Capital, in 1999. In 2001, the two recruited longtime tech executive Eric Schmidt to run the company as its CEO, with Brin becoming president of technology and Page, president of products, but with the duo continuing to make the corporation's important decisions.

In 2004, Google became a publicly-held corporation with its long-anticipated initial public stock offering. In August 2004, the corporation went public at an initial price of $85 per share, raising $1.67 billion. Since then, its shares have soared ever higher and higher, at least until 2008.

As its corporation mission, Goolge seeks "to organize the world's information and make it universally accessible and useful."[7] The corporation accounts for more than two thirds of all web searches in the United States and sells advertising in forty-three languages. Google provides its search engine service free of charge to anyone with an Internet connection, and generates revenue through an innovative advertising scheme, called AdWords and AdSense, that coordinates the advertisements it places on others' websites. Google dominates the search engine market because the model it developed maximizes comprehensiveness and relevancy in a way other search engines have been unable to match, at least to date. As a result, the firm serves a paragon of economic profitability, generating ever higher profits for its shareholders.

Building on the profitability of its search engine business, Google has positioned itself to become the powerhouse of the Internet economy. The company extended its reach into satellite mapping with Google Earth, a program created by Keyhole, Inc., a firm Google acquired in 2004, which allows users to get a birds-eye view of anywhere in the world. It spent $1 billion in March 2006 to acquire 5 percent of Time Warner's America Online unit, which enabled Google to sell ads on AOL. Its online payments system, Google Checkout, started in June 2006, allows registered users a fast and easy way to make purchases on the web by completing a credit card information form and subsequently entering only their username and password when making a purchase. In August 2006, it created a $900 million alliance with the social network site MySpace, owned by Fox Interactive Media, which allows MySpace users to search the site using Google's technology, and advertisers on MySpace get the benefit of AdWords and AdSense. It then bought YouTube, a video-sharing website, in November 2006 for $1.65 billion in Google stock, allowing the firm to become a major distributor of entertainment. In 2008, it acquired an online advertising firm, DoubleClick Inc., for $3.1 billion in cash, thereby pushing Google deeper into the business of placing electronic display ads on websites. Through these various acquisitions and investments, according to one commentator, "Google is this era's transformational computing platform and could be about to unseat Microsoft from its throne."[8]

Google's Corporate Philosophy and Philanthropy

In an open letter, titled "An Owner's Manual for Google's Shareholders" and attached to its 2004 initial public offering filing, Page delineated Google's core business and ethical principles. It began: "Google is not a conventional company. We do not intend to become one."[9] After setting forth the firms's corporate motto: "Don't be evil,"[10] he hoped its future products would have an even greater positive impact on the world. He asserted that the firm is committed to the public good, to improving the lives of as many people as possible, and to being trustworthy. To this end, Page also told potential investors that Google planned to contribute 1 percent of its equity and profits "in some form" to a charitable vehicle, at that time called the Google Foundation, he and Brin were in the process of establishing, thereby disclosing to potential shareholders they intended to fund philanthropy through the corporation. "We hope someday this institution may eclipse Google itself in overall world impact by ambitiously applying innovation and significant resources to the largest of the world's problems," Page wrote.[11]

The Creation of Google.org

With such lofty goals, it took the duo sometime to find a suitable philanthropic structure and areas of focus. Going beyond a traditional corporate foundation, Brin and Page took a far broader approach. In late 2004, the corporation adopted the name *Google.org* for its philanthropic endeavors.

Then in October 2005, Google Inc. formally established its philanthropic entity, Google.org, as a corporate unit, not a separate legal entity.[12] In keeping with their "1 percent" pledges, over a period as long as twenty years Brin and Page committed to donate to *Google.org*: 3 million of the firm's shares then (in late 2005) worth about nine hundred million dollars and 1 percent of Google's profits each year. Giving away 1 percent of its annual profits put the firm in line with the national average for corporate charitable donations. In general terms, funds derived from its shares and corporate profits would be divided between a tax exempt foundation to fund nonprofit entities and a vehicle designed to fund a broader range of initiatives, including investments in socially minded businesses and efforts to influence public policy.

Recognizing that philanthropy needs to build and scale social benefit organizations that last, in October 2005, Google Inc. donated $90 million in cash to fund the Google Foundation, a tax exempt 501(c)(3) organization previously formed in 2004. However, the firm indicated that it did not expect to make further donations to the foundation in the foreseeable future. The firm also allocated $175 million over the next three years as part of its 1 percent commitment for philanthropic activities across the *Google.org* spectrum, with some of these funds directed investments in for-profit ventures.

The Rationale for Google.org

Google Inc. will use the for-profit arm of *Google.org* for the bulk of its giving, thereby obtaining greater flexibility in how it deploys its funds. In devising the structure they created, Brin and Page believe that *Google.org*'s largely for-profit status would increase its range and flexibility. Even before organizing *Google.org*, they wrote, "[W]e believe we need to go beyond the traditional definition of a foundation and combine a variety of approaches—investing in socially progressive companies, making targeted philanthropic donations, influencing public policy, and more."[13] Any profits generated by investments in for-profit firms will be recycled back to *Google.org* and not flow to the back parent company. Nevertheless, some feel that Google Inc. might be tempted to do exactly this in the event of a severe general economic downturn or, if for some reason, the firm encounters financial difficulties. "It's possible the shareholders of Google might someday object, especially if we go into an economic depression and that money is needed to shore up the company," one observer noted.[14]

For Google Inc., *Google.org*'s range and flexibility has many dimensions. *Google.org* can decide what counts as a worthy cause, rather than following the IRS definition of an acceptable donee.

Freed from the constraints that limit the use of traditional foundation funds, following a strategy similar to the one adopted by Pierre Omidyar, as discussed in Chapter 4, *Google.org*'s for-profit arm will invest in companies that produce both social and environmental benefits and a financial return. It will fund startup and existing companies and also form partnerships with venture capitalists to tackle systemic problems. As Page stated, "For us, a lot of these things are investments [in for-profit businesses] just like normal business deals, but we don't really expect to make a lot of money right away. They aren't nonprofits, but they're less-profits. Maybe they'll take 10 years to pay." He continued, "There's a huge amount of money that exists in the 501(c)(3) structure, but we figure we can get some leverage by doing things out of that structure that other people aren't doing."[15] In other words, *Google.org* will invest in businesses having a potentially large social impact, but may not generate highest possible financial returns. Rather, these firms will help jump-start innovations that help solve social problems.

Google.org's for-profit status also will allow it to lobby for political causes without worrying about whether its efforts will exceed the federal limitations placed on such activities by foundations. Subject to making voluntary disclosures and meeting the requirements imposed by the U.S. Securities and Exchange Commission, the corporate structure will enable the firm to conceal *Google.org*'s investments and its other activities from public scrutiny. Apart from the Google Foundation, *Google.org* will not be required to make annual public disclosures to the Internal Revenue Service.

These various benefits come with trade-offs. Google Inc. will, of course, pay corporate taxes on the gains realized on the sale of its shares that go to fund *Google.org*. In contrast, if the corporation had contributed its shares to a foundation, it could have done so without being taxed on the gain and would have received a charitable contribution deduction. Any gain on the sale of its shares held by the foundation would be tax free. Also, any returns generated by the for-profit arm of *Google.org* are taxable as part of the corporation's income.

The Google Foundation and the Google Grants Program

Prior to 2008, the Google Foundation served as the more active branch of *Google.org*, perhaps forced by the federal requirement to spend 5 percent of its assets each year.[16] Some of the foundation's grants include: $1.7 million to TechnoServe, Inc., a nonprofit located in Norwalk, Connecticut, which sponsors business plan competitions in Central America and Africa, specifically national competitions in Ghana and Tanzania, with the winners receiving start-up business financing;[17] $2 million to the One Laptop Per Child Foundation, started by Nicholas Negropointe, co-founder of MIT's Media Lab, which developed a low price computer to give to children in the developing world;[18] $2 million to the Seva Foundation, to support programs to prevent blindness and restore eyesight in Third World nations.[19]

The Google Foundation gave $5.2 million to the Acumen Fund to support its entrepreneurial approaches to addressing global poverty and providing services to the poor, mainly to fund its fellows program. According to Sheryl Sandberg, "It's addressing the critical needs of the world's poor, but in much more of a venture capital mode: to use seed money to address the world's problems and to do so in a sustainable way."[20]

Acumen, a nonprofit venture capital fund, profiled in Chapter 5, among other activities, annually sponsors eight young professionals to work with its companies in Asia and Africa. The Acumen Fund Fellows Program offers each participant the opportunity to use their skills to effect social change through its portfolio organizations and also to build the expertise and relationships that will enable them to develop into global leaders. After two months of intensive training in New York in valuation techniques, business models, and risk analysis, the fellows serve a nine-month field assignment in Asia and Africa with an Acumen portfolio investment and then return to New York for a final month to share their experiences and exchange lessons learned.[21]

Two other Google-Acumen projects are noteworthy. Google's software engineers designed a system to track Acumen's investments. Acumen also moved its offices to a floor in Google's Manhattan building.

Google.org also includes the Google Grants program, which the corporation established in 2003. A traditional philanthropic effort, the Google Grants offer nonprofits around the world the company's marketing expertise. Approximately $200 million in AdWords advertising has been given free of charge to some 3,300 nonprofit organizations worldwide to help them connect with their target audiences. Google has given these free ads to nonprofits it feels are worthy in various areas, such as human rights, environmental causes, and the alleviation of global poverty. Nonprofits supported include the Grameen Foundation USA, Doctors Without Borders, and the Make-a-Wish Foundation.[22] As a result of the 2006 settlement of a lawsuit, *Google.org* has increased the funds devoted to the Google Grants program.[23]

Appointing Google.org's Executive Director

Google.org gradually found its focus, after Brin and Page selected an executive director, who, in turn, added new team members to spearhead strategic initiatives in its philanthropic efforts. Less than six months after creating *Google.org*, in February 2006, Brin and Page named Larry Brilliant, a counterculture figure, the executive director of *Google.org*.[24]

After receiving his medical degree, Brilliant studied for two years with a famous Hindu guru. In 1973, shortly before the guru's death, he told Brilliant to use his medical skills to eradicate smallpox, which was then devastating India. Brilliant joined a UN team that worked through India inoculating people against smallpox. By 1980, the World Health Organization declared smallpox eradicated in India.

Returning to the United States, Brilliant led both international nonprofit organizations and technology companies. In 1979, he started the Seva Foundation, which focuses on preventing and curing blindness in Asia and Africa. In 1985, he co-founded The Well, an online community, which still exists as part of *Salon.com*. In the 1990s and early 2000s, he ran several high tech companies. From 1988 to 2002, Brilliant served as CEO of SoftNet Systems Inc., a global broadband Internet service company, which morphed into an insurance holding company in 2002. He then became the interim CEO of Cometa Networks, a joint venture of Intel, IBM, and AT&T, which sought to develop a national Wi-Fi system before it was dissolved in 2003.

Google.org's Activities

Google.org's progress to date has been far slower compared to its parent's breakneck growth in revenues, staff, and business reach. It took Brin and Page some time to find specific areas of interest for their corporate philanthropy. In Google Inc.'s 2005 Annual Report, Brin and Page spelled out their philanthropic focus: "... [W]e set up and funded the Google Foundation [in October 2005] and refined its focus areas to providing sustainable development for the world's poorest citizens and harnessing people, money, and scientific resources to combat climate change."[25]

As the philanthropic process evolved beyond the creation of a corporate foundation, by the spring of 2007 *Google.org* initially narrowed its focus to three major areas the unit felt represented significant global problems: climate change (seemingly a special obsession of Brin and Page); global public health; and economic development and poverty alleviation (a passion of Sheryl Sandberg), the last two mirroring the efforts of the Gates Foundation. More specifically, *Google.org* began by exploring the best approaches to mitigate the impact of climate change, particularly on the world's poor, by reducing greenhouse gas emissions, improving energy efficiency, decreasing dependence on petroleum, and promoting clean energy technologies. In the area of global public health, reflecting a pet project of Brilliant, it sought to "better predict, prevent and eradicate communicable diseases through better access to and use of information." It hoped to assist in developing scalable, sustainable solutions to poverty through a focus on economic growth propelled by the private sector and improving the access to information by the poor.[26]

Prior to 2008. Google.org's most notable efforts centered on one of its preliminary core missions, namely, alleviating climate change, by accelerating the commercialization of plug-in autos and make renewable energy cheaper than coal. Its program to Accelerate the Commercialization of Plug-in Vehicles (RechargeIT), announced in June 2007, aims to decrease carbon dioxide emissions, cut petroleum consumption, and stabilize the electricity grid by stimulating the adoption of plug-in hybrid gasoline-electric vehicles as well as vehicle-to-grid technology.[27] The RechargeIT effort relies on plug-in hybrid autos that draw power from a combination of an electric battery and gasoline engine. Having bigger, more powerful batteries and a long cord that could plug into a normal 120-volt household outlet, these vehicles could travel 20 to 40 miles using little or no gasoline. On short commuter runs, this type of hybrid car would not need to use its gasoline engine. With most Americans driving less than thirty-five miles per day, they could drive almost exclusively on electricity, with gasoline as a safety net.

To implement these goals, *Google.org* modified several hybrid gas-electric autos to run partly on electricity from the existing power grid. These modifications, which consisted of using extra batteries to hold energy distributed by a power company, allowed the cars to go up to

75 miles on a gallon of gasoline. Also, with advice from Pacific Gas & Electric Co., Google equipped one modified vehicle to give electricity back to the grid through vehicle-to-grid recharging stations.

The firm has also acquired plug-in hybrid vehicles for its corporate fleet. These cars are equipped with a second, high-capacity battery. By charging the battery through a wall outlet when a vehicle is not in use, the modified hybrids can get upward of seventy miles per gallon.

In 2007, *Google.org* gave $1 million in grants to various organizations that are encouraging the adoption of plug-in hybrid cars. As part of its plan to facilitate the development of various types of plug-in cars through research and testing, *Google.org* also sponsored a $10 million competition to accelerate the development of battery technology, plug-in hybrid gas-electric engines, fully electric plug-in vehicles (called PHEVs), and vehicles capable of returning stored energy to a power grid. If the later effort becomes commercially feasible, with vehicle-to-grid technology, called V2G, fleets of hybrid cars could recharge at night when electricity demand is lower and supply a grid during the day, thereby helping avert serious blackouts. To advance the technology around plug-ins, *Google. org*, according to Dan Reicher, the director of its climate and energy initiatives, "decided to take a different route, a public request for investment proposals. We wanted to look beyond the usual players, bring attention to a critical area, and catalyze competition and innovation."[28] *Google.org* will invest $500,000 to $2 million in selected for-profit firms.

Significant barriers exist to building a new generation of hybrid engines capable of getting 100 miles per gallon using gasoline and alternative fuels. Plug-in electric hybrids would require more powerful batteries that charge more quickly than the existing batteries. The goal of developing a fuel-efficient plug-in hybrid, with mileage of 100 miles per gallon, remains a worthy objective for *Google.org*. This type of engine would reduce U.S. dependence on foreign oil and help alleviate greenhouse gas emissions. As Reicher noted, "If we can crack the code on plug-in vehicles, I think it will be transformative."[29] However, what can *Google. org* do that Toyota and Honda, among others, cannot?[30] And, at what cost to Google in future years? Does Google have too much cash on its hands? Will the firm spread itself too thin as it branches beyond online advertising?

Beyond a focus on more fuel efficient autos, *Google.org* sponsored the Climate Savers Computing Initiative, which aims to reduce greenhouse gas emissions by making computers more energy efficient. It also took advantage of its for-profit status by lobbying the public sector in the U.S. on the issue of climate change. Efforts championed by *Google.org*'s executives included the proposed federal Energy Efficiency Resource Standard and Renewable Portfolio Standard and the California "Global Warming Solutions Act of 2006."[31]

In November 2007, Google Inc. announced plans to get into the business of finding limitless, renewable energy sources. In a high-profile initiative, *Google.org* expects to invest hundreds of millions of dollars to develop and help stimulate the creation of renewable energy technologies, such as solar, geothermal, and wind power, that, without public subsides, are cheaper than coal-generated power. Based in its parent's newly created renewable-energy research and development group, the initiative is called RE<C, denoting renewable energy is cheaper than coal. The firm also stated that *Google.org* would invest in alternative energy start-ups and fledgling firms, particularly those that have the best chance of successfully developing the lowest-per-unit-cost renewable techniques. Without offering details, *Google.org* indicated it was working with two companies offering promising, scalable energy technologies. The first, eSolar Inc., uses thousands of small mirrors to concentrate sunlight and generate steam that powers electric generators. The second, Makani Power Inc., is developing high-altitude wind-power systems.[32]

Google.org's moves could transform the business mix of its parent and lead to the firm becoming a major player in the energy sector. In announcing the RE<C initiative, Page stated:

> With talented technologists, great partners and significant investments, we hope to rapidly push forward. Our goal is to produce one gigawatt of renewable energy capacity [to power a city the size of San Francisco] that is cheaper than coal. We are optimistic this can be done in years, not decades. If we meet this goal and large-scale renewable deployments are cheaper than coal, the world will have the option to meet a substantial portion of electricity needs from renewable sources and significantly reduce carbon emissions. We expect this would be a good business for us as well.[33]

In short, Google Inc. could become a business rival of some coal companies.

As a second focus, *Google.org* began a campaign to alleviate public health problems in Third World countries. Building on Brilliant's idea that won him the TED (Technology, Entertainment, Design) Prize in 2006, not unexpectedly, *Google.org* donated an initial startup grant of $975,000 to establish an independent nonprofit group, InSTEDD (Innovative Support to Emergencies and Disasters).[34] The group that Brilliant helped establish seeks to harness technology to develop an early detection, prevention, and response system to natural disasters and major public health crises. By applying software and other technology to improve the flow of information among organizations fighting these problems, *Google. org* believes that better data and analytic systems are key to identifying these potential hot spots.

Finally, in the field of global economic development, *Google.org* began to undertake three exploratory initiatives to understand and address information asymmetries in order to enhance the conditions for the more equitable economic growth and to improve the access to and quality of essential services in the developing world. One initiative focused on supporting the development and growth of small and medium enterprises in Africa. A second sought to identify and implement critical information platforms which could stimulate better access to both capital and markets for entrepreneurs and enterprises in the developing world. The third explored using information as a lever to improve the provision of essential services to the poor.[35]

2008 and Onward. Then in January 2008, reflecting its stepped-up activity, Google unveiled $26 million in new grants and investments and outlined how it will focus up to $175 million in grants and investments over the next three years.[36] In addition to developing more advanced hybrid cars and finding renewable energy sources that are less expensive than coal, its major five-to-ten-year initiatives will focus on efforts to: create systems to help predict and prevent disease pandemics; empower the poor with information about public services; and create jobs by investing in small and medium-size businesses in the developing world. These initiatives show Brin, Page, and Brilliant's interest in projects where they can bring the firm's information management and engineering prowess to bear on complex problems. As Brilliant noted:

> These five initiatives are our attempt to address some of the hard problems we as a world need to face in the coming decade. We have chosen them both we think solving them will make a better, fairer, safer world for our children and grandchildren —and the children and grandchildren of people all over the world—but also because we feel that these core initiatives fit well with Google's core strengths, especially its innovative technologies and it talented engineers and other Googlers, who are really our most valuable assets.[37]

As part of its "Develop Renewable Energy Cheaper Than Coal" initiative, *Google.org* invested $10 million in eSolar Inc., a closely-held firm, which is working on utility-scale solar power. It had also invested $10 million in Makani Power Inc. to support research and development on high-altitude wind energy technologies.[38]

Its "Predict and Prevent" initiative focuses on strengthening early warning systems globally to detect a disease before it becomes a pandemic or a drought before it becomes a famine. To attain this goal, *Google.org* made an additional $5 million grant to InSTEED. It also gave $2.5 million to the Nuclear Threat Initiative's Global Health and Security Initiative to improve the surveillance of biological threats in Southeast Asia.[39]

As part of its "Inform and Empower to Improve Public Services" initiative, *Google.org* seeks to support efforts to provide parties in the Third world with information about public services, such as education, healthcare, and infrastructure. For example, it gave $2 million to Pratham, an Indian nongovernmental organization, to create a nationwide annual report on education.[40] It also awarded $765,000 to the Center for Budget and Policy Studies, a Bangalore-based analysis group, to establish a Budget Information Service to improve local planning in India.

Google.org also aims to "Fuel the Growth of Small and Medium-Sized Enterprises" in the developing world. Striving to encourage the middle level of financing between microcredit organizations and traditional banks and capital markets, it seeks to: reduce the transaction costs for outsiders to invest in these businesses; help create funds that buy stakes in the businesses and provide investors with an exit strategy; and invest, directly and indirectly, in such businesses. Seemingly reflecting the view that Gates and Omidyar, among others, had preempted the microfinance field, Brilliant stated, "No country has ever emerged from poverty because of microcredit. Jobs make that possible. China did it with manufacturing, India did it with outsourced call centers."[41]

To stimulate jobs, through the growth of small- and medium-sized businesses, TechnoServe, previously funded by the Google Foundation, received a $3 million grant. The funds would enable TechnoServe to provide general support to expand its efforts to facilitate enterprises, spur job creation, strengthen poverty alleviation programs in Africa, and continue to support the development and implementation for business plan competitions in Ghana and Tanzania.[42]

Looking to the future, Brin and Page understand that *Google.org*'s activities might adversely impact Google's online advertising business. Viewing Google as a rival, energy firms might cut back on purchasing Google ads. Also, public officials unhappy with *Google.org*'s activities might use their legislative or regulatory powers to punish the firm. Seemingly, Google considered these economic and political risks. According to Brilliant, "It's an experiment to a philanthropically oriented organization that's part of the [profit and loss] of Google."[43]

Much about the future impact of *Google.org* remains uncertain. The effort to sift through more than one thousand possible ideas made *Google.org* slow to get moving, particularly on the for-profit side, but it is clear that the unit has embraced a new model that combines philanthropy with investment. Similar to the Gates Foundation, *Google.org* approaches its projects as a venture capitalist. It looks for talented people with big ideas, and will back them with substantial funds. Both the Gates Foundation and *Google.org* expect most of their projects will fail, but they anticipate one or two important breakthroughs.

Brin and Page's assertion that they hope *Google.org* eclipses Google Inc. in its positive impact on the world may seem like bombast, but if their new approach to philanthropy delivers in the way they expect, *Google.org* has a chance of achieving this goal. However, the question remains whether Brin and Page ought to make donations and investments personally, as Gates, Omidyar, Skoll, and Case have done, rather than using Google Inc.'s shares and its profits.

Notes

1. Google Inc., "Letter From The Founders: 'An Owner's Manual' For Google's Shareholders," U.S. Securities and Exchange Commission, Form S-1, Registration Statement, filed April 29, 2004, i.
2. Jennifer 8. Lee, "A Charity with an Unusual Interest in the Bottom Line," *New York Times*, November 13, 2006, F1.
3. Luisa Kroll and Allison Fass, "The World's Billionaires," *Forbes* 179:6 (March 26, 2007): 104-208, at 154.
4. Luisa Kroll with Matthew Miller, "Billionaire Rankings: Index," *Forbes* 181:6 (March 24, 2008): 146-160, at 148 and 156.
5. For background on Brin and Page I have drawn on David A. Vise and Mark Malseed, *The Google Story* (New York: Bantam Dell, 2005); John Battelle, *The Search: How Google and Its Rivals Rewrote the Rules of Business and Transformed Our Culture* (New York: Portfolio, 2005); John Heileman, "Journey to the (Revolutionary, Evil-Hating, Cash-Crazy, and Possibly Self-Destructive) Center of Google," *Men.Style.com*, March 2005 <http:men.style.com/gq/features> (August 24, 2007); Michael Specter, "Search and Deploy," *New Yorker* 76:13 (May 29, 2000): 88-95.
6. Vise and Malseed, *Google*, 24.
7. Google Inc., U.S. Securities and Exchange Commission Form 10-K, March 1, 2007, 1.
8. Elinor Mills, "Google Builds an Empire to Rival Microsoft," *ZDNet News*, September 21, 2005 <http://news.zdnet.com/2100-9588_22-5875433.html> (August 24, 2007).
9. Google Inc., "Letter From The Founders," I.
10. *Ibid.*, vi.
11. *Ibid.*, vi.
12. Sheryl Sandberg, "About Google.org," October 11, 2005 <http://googleblog.blogspot.com/2005/10/about-googleorg.html> (April 8, 2007). I have also drawn

on Chris Gaither, "Google Sets Aside $1 billion for Causes," *Los Angeles Times*, October 12, 2005, C2; David A. Vise, "Google Starts Up Philanthropy Campaign," *Washington Post*, October 12, 2005, D4; Saul Hansell, "Google Earmarks $265 Million for Charity and Social Causes," *New York Times*, October 12, 2005, C9; Verne Kopytoff, "Google Lays out Plan to Change the World," *San Francisco Chronicle*, October 12, 2005, C1; Margaret Steen, "Google Sets up Fund to Do Good," *San Jose Mercury News*, October 12, 2005, C1; Kevin J. Delaney, "Google Outlines Philanthropic Plan," Wall Street Journal Online, October 12, 2005.

13. Google Inc., "Annual Report," 2004, Sergey Brin and Larry Page, "Founders Letter."
14. Katie Hafner, "Philanthropy Google's Way," *New York Times*, September 14, 2006, A1.
15. Natalie Ghidotti, "The New Wave of Philanthropy," *NonProfit Times* 21:2 (January 15, 2007): 1, 4-5, at 5.
16. Jim Hopkins, "Google Makes Good on Plans for Charity," *USA Today*, October 12, 2005, 5B.
17. Nick Railston-Brown, "TechnoService Announces Entrepreneur Development Program Winners in Ghana," September 21, 2006 <http://googleblog.blogspot.com/2006/09/technoserve> (February 19, 2008); Nick Railston-Brown, "TechnoServe Update," March 30, 2006 <http://googleblog.blogspot.com/2006/03/technoserve> (February 19, 2008); Bruce McNamer, "TechnoServe Comes to Google," January 21, 2006 <http://googleblog.blogspot.com/2006/01/technoserve> (February 19, 2008). See also Richard Lee, "Technoserve, Google Search for Excellence," *Stamford Advocate* (Stamford, CT), November 17, 2006, 1; Richard Lee, "Norwalk Nonprofit Recognized as One of Best in World," *Stamford Advocate* (Stamford, CT), July 21, 2007, A1.
18. David Kirkpatrick, "I'd Like To Teach The World To Type," *Fortune* 152:11 (November 28, 2005): 63-64. For background on Nicholas Negroponte's laptop see Steve Stecklow, "Laptop Program for Kids in Poor Countries Team Up with Microsoft's Windows," *Wall Street Journal*, May 16, 2007, C1; Steve Lohr, "Microsoft Joins Efforts for Laptops for Children," *New York Times*, May 16, 2008, C1; Steve Stecklow, "Laptop-Project Founder Faults Intel," *Wall Street Journal*, January 5-6, 2008, A4; John Markoff, "Intel Ends Deal to Give Computer to Children," *New York Times*, January 5, 2008, B3; Steve Stecklow and James Bandler, "A Little Laptop with Big Ambitions," *Wall Street Journal*, November 24-25, 2007, A1; Leslie Walker, "On a Laptop Mission for Kids," *Washington Post*, November 18, 2007, F6. David Pogue, "$100 Laptop A Bargain at $200," *New York Times*, October 4, 2007, C1; Steve Lohr, "Buy a Laptop for a Child, Get Another Laptop Free," *New York Times*, September 24, 2007, C1; Jessica E. Vascellaro, "Laptop Charity Seeks Help from Home Market," *Wall Street Journal*, September 24, 2007, B9; Lee Gomes, "Making a Difference, One Laptop a Child," *Wall Street Journal*, July 17, 2007, B4; John Markoff, "For $150, Third-World Laptop Stirs a Big Debate," *New York Times*, November 30, 2006, A1; David Kirkpatrick, "This PC Wants to Save the World," *Fortune* 154:9 (October 30, 2006): 82; Kevin Maney, "Gates see Cellphones, Not Laptops, as Way to Help Third World," *USA Today*, February 1, 2006, 3 B.
19. *Google.org*, "Grants," and Seva Foundation, "Spirit of Service," Spring 06, 4.
20. Lee, "A Charity with an Unusual Interest in the Bottom Line."
21. Acumen Fund, Press Release, "Acumen Fund Initiative Will Develop 'Entrepreneurial Bench' in Fight Against Global Poverty," May 24, 2006.

22. Google Grants, "In-Kind Advertising for Non-Profit Organizations" <http://www.goolge.com/grants> (April 19, 2007).
23. The settlement in Lane's Gifts and Collectibles, L.L.C. et al v. Yahoo! Inc. et al, Final Order and Judgment Approving Settlement, Certifying Class For Settlement Purposes, Awarding Class Counsel Attorney's Fee And Dismissing Action With Prejudice, Case No. CV-2005-52-1 Circuit Court Of Miller County, Arkansas, July 26, 2006, required Google to issue AdWords credits to nonprofits of not more than $30 million.
24. Google Inc., Press Release, "Google Names Larry Brilliant as Executive Director of *Google.org*," February 22, 2006. See also Dan Fost, "Foundation Names Larry Brilliant Chief," *San Francisco Chronicle*, February 22, 2006, C1; Jim Hopkins, "Google Signs on Do-Good Doctor to Head Charity," *USA Today*, February 22, 2006, 5B; Patrick Hoge, "Profile: Larry Brilliant," *San Francisco Chronicle*, February 24, 2006, A1; Hafner, "Philanthropy Google's Way."
25. Google Inc., "Annual Report," 2005, Sergey Brin and Larry Page, "Founders Letter," 8.
26. *Google.org*, "Welcome to *Google.org*—the Philanthropy Arm of Google" <http://google.org> (April 19, 2007).
27. Google Press Center, Press Release, "Google Launches RechargeIT Plug-In Hybrid Car Initiative and Unveils Solar Installation," June 18, 2007; *Google.org*, "*RechargeIT.org*: A *Google.org* Project," <http:www.google.org/recharge/overview.html> (February 24, 2008); *Google.org*, "RechargeIT" <http:www.google.org/climate.html> (August 24, 2007); and Dan Reicher, "A clean energy update," June 18, 2007 <http://googleblog.blogspot.com /2007/06clean-energy-update.html>(September 2, 2007). The various grants made by the RechargeIT program are detailed in *Google.org*, "Grants and Investments" <http://www.google.org/projects.html> (February 19, 2008). See also Felicity Barringer and Matthew L. Wald, "Google and Utility to Test Hybrids That Sell Back Power," *New York Times*, June 19, 2007, C3; Todd Woody, "Have You Driven a Fjord Lately?," *Business 2.0* 8:7 (August 2007): 54-59; Steve Bryant, "Google Goes for the Green," CIO Insight.com, June 19, 2007 <LexisNexis>; David Lazarus, "Google's Future is Green," *San Francisco Chronicle*, June 20, 2007, C1; Martin Zimmerman, "Google Invests in Plug-In Hybrid Cars," *Los Angeles Times*, June 19, 2007, C3; James R. Healey, "Google Gets Hybrid Plug-In Hybrid Cars," *USA Today*, June 19, 2007, 1B; Jim Motavalli, "The Real Power of the Prius," *New York Times* (Late Edition), September 2, 2007, Section 10, 5; Jim Motavalli, "Hybrids with a Power Cord," *New York Times*, October 1, 2006, Section 12, 6; and Marianne Lavelle, "A Plug For Hybrids," *U.S. News & World Report* 141:13 (October 9, 2006): 45-46.
28. Keith Schneider, "Win Fabulous Prizes, All in the Name of Innovation," *New York Times*, November 12, 2007, 33.
29. Marianne Lavelle, "Power Revolution," *U.S. News & World Report* 143:16 (November 5, 2007): 46-53, at 53.
30. For the auto makers' activities, see Joseph B. White and Norihiko Shirouzu, "Hybrid or All-Electric? Car Makers Take Sides," *Wall Street Journal*, October 24, 2007, A13.
31. *Google.org*, "Climate Change" <http://www.google.org/climate.html> (August 24, 2007) and Prepared Statement of Dan W. Reicher, Director, Climate Change and Energy Initiatives, *Google.org* in Hearing Before Committee on Energy and Natural Resources, United States Senate, *Advanced Energy Technologies*, S. Hrq. 110-63, 110th Congress, 1st Session, March 7, 2007, 6-13.

32. Google Press Center, Press Release, "Google's Goal: Renewable Energy Cheaper than Coal," November 27, 2007. See also Brad Stone, "A Subsidiary Charts Google's Next Frontier: Renewable Energy," *New York Times*, November 28, 2007, C3; Rebecca Smith and Kevin J. Delaney, "Google's Electicity Initiative," *Wall Street Journal*, November 28, 2007; Marianne Lavelle, "On the Record," *U.S. News & World Report* 143:20 (December 10, 2007): 60.
33. Google Press Center, Press Release, "Google's Goal," November 27, 2007 and Larry Page "Towards More Renewable Energy," November 27, 2007 <*http://googleblog.blogspot.com/2007/11/towards-more-renewable-e*> (February 24, 2008).
34. *Google.org*, "Global Public Health" <*http://www.google.org/publichealth.html*> (September 2, 2007).
35. *Google.org*, "Global Economic Development" <*http://www.google.org/development.html*> (September 2, 2007).
36. *Google.org*, Press Release, "*Google.org* Announces Core Initiatives to Combat Climate Change, Poverty and Emerging Threats," January 17, 2008. See also Kevin J. Delaney, "Google: From 'Don't Be Evil' to How To Do Good," *Wall Street Journal*, January 18, 2008, B1; Harriet Rubin, "Google's Searches Now Include Ways to Make a Better World," *New York Times*, January 18, 2008, C1; Verne Kopytoff, "*Google.org* Invests, Grants $26 Million," *San Francisco Chronicle*, January 18, 2008, C1; Chloe Albanesius, "Google Detail Humanitarian Funding Effort," *PC Magazine*, January 17, 2008 <*http://www.pcmag.com/article2/0,2704,2250/6/,00asp*>.
37. *Google.org*, Press Release, "*Google.org* Announces Core Initiatives."
38. *Google.org*, "Grants and Investments," January 2008 <*http://www.google.org/projects/html*> (February 24, 2008).
39. Global Health and Security Initiative, Press Release, "NTI's Global Health and Security Program Receives Major Grant from Google Foundation," January 17, 2008.
40. Pratham USA, Press Release, "Google Awards $2 Million to Pratham for ASER," n.d.
41. Rubin, "Google's Searches Now Include." See also James Surowiecki, "What Microloans Miss," *New Yorker* 84:5 (March 17, 2008): 35.
42. TechnoServe, Press Release, "TechnoServe Receives a Grant from *Google.org* for International Development," January 17, 2008. In 2008, TechnoServe also received a $46.9 million grant from the Gates Foundation to help thousands of small-scale farmers improve the quality of their coffee and enhance their income. Mark Ginocchio, "TechnoServe Aids African Farmers," *Stamford Advocate* (Stamford, CT), April 26, 2008, A1.
43. Delany, "Google."

8

Conclusion

The new generation of wealthy donors, as exemplified by the tech billionaires profiled in this book, strive to apply their capital, philosophies, and business skills in an attempt to achieve social goals. They recognize that global problems—disease and poverty—are so complex as to require new organizational forms and new types of collaborations, thereby blurring the lines between business and philanthropy as well as between the public and private sectors. In bringing their own skills and their own approaches to philanthropy, they seek to maximize social returns, in so doing begin to solve social problems, and hopefully stimulate innovative public sector solutions.

The impact of the new philanthropists is distinct from the old philanthropists. Reflecting Bill Gate's entrepreneurial background, his foundation has spurred changes in how philanthropy operates, particularly among the older megafoundations. Bill Gates has also called for a revision of capitalism, what he calls "creative capitalism," which rests on the recognition donors may achieve. The question, however, remains: how to harness the vitality of capitalism to meet social needs? A socially-driven end with a capitalist means may be carried out in the marketplace. Thus, in the future, social businesses may possibly be funded, in part, by foundations and social stock markets.

New Philanthropists Reshape Older and Contemporary Philanthropy

By the late twentieth century, many megafoundations had become ossified. Going so far as wanting to change the system that produced social ills, over the past forty years or so, "activist" foundations put their funds in the service of an array of "liberal" causes, yet social problems, domestically and overseas, persist. Sclerotic, bureaucratic, secretive, and drifting, traditional philanthropy, seen as insufficiently businesslike, had become more marginal in its impact.[1]

The winds of change are now blowing at both the Carnegie Corporation and Rockefeller Foundation, among other giant foundations.[2] Spurred on by the upstart, more businesslike approach of the Gates Foundation, among other tech billionaires' foundations, megafoundations are striving to consolidate and integrate the number of their programs and rationalize them, focusing on a few, well-chosen areas and sticking to them. They are looking to increase their efficiency, through the sharing of expertise and, in general, having a clearer focus. They increasingly seek to fund big, strategic projects, often cutting across programmatic areas. In addition to conducting extensive due diligence, setting clear expectations about how grantees will spend funds, and becoming more results-oriented, they are demanding more information from recipients on how the funds they provide are spent and are striving to measure the impact of their grants. With foundations taking the position that the return on grants should be both tangible and measurable, transparency and accountability increasingly serve as transforming watchwords.

Beyond their impact on older foundations, it is unclear, however, whether the wealth accumulating skills of the tech billionaires can transfer to problem-solving on a grand scale. Those featured in this book have a genuine social consciousness and want to make a difference in overcoming today's problems, while still alive. They are focusing on giving to achieve measurable results and seek accountability for their funds.

It is uncertain whether the new rich, who made their money very quickly, through technology, and are often intoxicated with their own brilliance, can quickly achieve results and change the world. Because social problems are deeper and far more complex than inventing a new software program, they may fall flat on their faces. Even with the analytical screening of potential grantees and the development of better measures of assessing the impact of grant and investment recipients, only a limited number of talented social entrepreneurs and viable social purpose businesses exist. With a dearth of scalable models, nonprofit grantees and for-profit businesses may be unable to absorb increased donations or investments, grow quickly, and last.

Bill Gates's Vision For Capitalism

In January 2008, Bill Gates espoused a modification of capitalism. Whether Gates will have a huge influence among his super-wealthy peers remains uncertain.

In a speech at The World Economic forum in Davos, Switzerland, he called for a "creative capitalism" that would use market forces to address the needs of developing countries he feels are being ignored. Returning to his concern about inequality, discussed in Chapter 3, he is troubled that advances in technology, health care, and education tend to bypass the poor in the Third World.

As the key to his vision of creative capitalism, Gates wants companies to establish businesses that focus on providing goods and services for the poor. Rephrasing the call for corporate responsibility, he stated:

> Such a system would have a twin mission: making profits and also improving lives of those who don't fully benefit from today's market forces. For sustainability we need to use profit incentives wherever we can. At the same time, profits are not always possible when business tries to serve the very poor. In such cases there needs to be another incentive, and that incentive is recognition. Recognition enhances a company's reputation and appeals to customers; above all, it attracts good people to an organization. As such, recognition triggers a market-based reward for good behavior...
>
> The challenge here is to design a system where market incentives, including profits and recognition, drive those principles to do more for the poor.
>
> Creative capitalism takes this interest in the fortunes of others and ties it to our interest in our own ways that help advance both. This hybrid engine of self-interest and concern for others can serve a much wider circle of people than can be reached by self-interest or caring alone.[3]

Gates seems to want to persuade for-profit companies to meet the needs of the globe's poor by boosting their "recognition" factor, using corporate philanthropy. The "recognition" factor may spur the energy conservation efforts of *Google.org*, as analyzed in Chapter 7; however, for businesses that do not enjoy a monopoly or dominant competitive position of a Microsoft or Google, recognition has proven a weak motivator compared to profit, for example, measured by the giving by American corporate philanthropy to the developing world. Furthermore, in the midst of fierce global competition, most corporate executives find it harder than ever to think beyond their income statements and balance sheets.

Rather than philanthropists trying to pick which goods and services will serve as a nation's growth engine, let microfinance organizations fund budding entrepreneurs. Many of these for-profit capitalists will lift themselves out of poverty; some may embark on their own decentralized path marked by greater success for their firms and even for their nation.

Another key to Gates's plan turns on businesses dedicating their top innovators' time to help lift people out of poverty. This approach, he feels, is more powerful than traditional corporate donations or offering employees' time off to volunteer. However, economic freedom and a lessening of corruption and stifling bureaucracy in Third World nations form, in my opinion, the best path to prosperity. The steep economic and social inequities Gates sees in his travels around the world, especially in Africa, come more from corruption and the absence of capitalist principles, not capitalism. The most innovative, the most compassionate corporate employees and executives face a difficult path to bring prosperity to impoverished, developing nations marked by corruption and statist, non-market economies. It would be better to direct brainpower to examine the barriers—political and social—that block entrepreneurial activity in the Third World and strive to develop ways to remove them.

As we assess various approaches to alleviate global poverty, many return to and are persuaded by the timeless advice of Andrew Carnegie. In his 1889 essay, "The Gospel of Wealth," Carnegie wrote that donors ought to use their fortunes on organizations that provide "the ladders upon which the aspiring can rise."[4] In his day, Carnegie funded libraries. Today, Gates and Omidyar, among the tech billionaires, back microenterprises as a key poverty alleviation strategy. Through capitalism, self-employment, and the growth of profit-maximizing small businesses that create goods and services and sell them on a local level, the number of people who cannot afford food and health care for themselves and their children is much smaller than it used to be.

The Social Business Concept

Beyond Bill Gates's concept of corporate social responsibility for for-profit businesses, beyond what nonprofit organizations and the public sector and its enterprises have traditionally done, a new sector—social business—is emerging, driven by social purpose.

Many entities and individuals may facilitate the growth of social businesses. Some foundations may create social business investment funds to support good works. Some young BBAs and MBAs may launch social enterprises, thereby using their skills to tackle serious social problems. Some wealth holders, such as those profiled in this book as well as other corporate executives, may fund social businesses as a means to implement meaningful change in the world. Some who made their money in profit-maximizing businesses as well as the children of successful business families who wish to help the poor in a socially beneficial and environmentally sustainable manner may find social enterprises a useful vehicle. Beyond these groups, social businesses would generally provide a means for the caring side of those who want to harness the power of private entities to facilitate social benefits through the market mechanism.[5]

Calling capitalism only "half developed"[6] because it focuses on the profit-oriented side of humans, not on the satisfaction derived from helping others, Nobel laureate Muhammad Yunus has taken the lead in advancing the social business concept.[7] Yunus foresees the growth of what he calls a social enterprise. It is a business which aims to do good, to change peoples' lives, and make a difference in the world. It is a sustainable, non-loss, non-divided-paying type of business entity which seeks to solve social, healthcare, and environmental problems, among others, using the economic marketplace.

A social business represents a sustainable, self-sufficient enterprise. Unlike a charity, it would not need new infusions of funds each year from donors as well as the public sector to maintain its operations and run one or more of its programs.[8] According to Yunus, if a social business generates a profit, it would stay in the entity to expand its outreach and improve the quality of its goods and services, but not go to investors in the form of dividends or other types of distributions. Investors would recoup their investment over a long payback period, say ten or twenty years, and could then reinvest in the same or a different social business.

Beyond talking about social businesses, Yunus has implemented a joint venture project, Grameen Danone Foods Ltd., in Bangladesh.[9] Yunus created this enterprise, the world's first multinational social business, to help solve a critical social problem—childhood malnutrition—by developing, with his joint venture partner, a new yogurt product especially for children. As Yunus put it, "Instead of making fancy yogurt for the rich, we are creating fortified yogurt for malnourished children."[10]

The joint venture between the Grameen Bank and Groupe Danone SA, a French-based multinational food company, seeks to improve child nutrition through a sustainable business model.[11] Aware that ill-health and poverty are interrelated, the joint venture puts micronutrients, such as vitamins and minerals, into yogurt, which it sells to the parents of nutritionally-deprived children, initially in a remote rural area of Bangladesh. So the poor can afford the product, it is made and sold for about eight cents a cup. The cost is set at a level so that impoverished families can buy two yogurts per week for each of their children.

The Grameen-Danone fifty-fifty joint venture serves as a model of social business, although departing in some respects from Yunus's ideal.

Danone provided one half of the start-up capital; the Grameen companies, the other half. To fund its share as well as provide capital for the expansion of the joint venture and other social businesses, Danone created a new money market mutual fund, Investment Company with Variable Capital, Danone Communities Fund, with 10 percent of its assets allocated to and invested in social enterprises. The firm gave its shareholders the option to invest in the fund if they wished. Other investors included institutions and the general public in France.

As a nonloss venture, Grameen-Danone is not designed to operate in the red; rather it will hopefully generate a small surplus. Under the joint venture agreement, each partner can recoup its capital investment after three years and thereafter receive a distribution equal to 1 percent on its original investment. The token dividend would serve to recognize publicly the ownership of the venture and allow Danone to show a figure on its balance sheet. Any additional profits would stay with the business so it could expand into other communities in Bangladesh, thereby replicating the model and helping more people. As a sustainable, self-supporting business, it would run by itself, unlike charities, which require regular capital infusions.

Over the next decade, the Grameen-Danone joint venture, if successful, plans to build fifty small, labor-intensive plants throughout Bangladesh, rather than one large, automated factory, emphasizing both social benefits and environmental sustainability. Using a community-focused model, each factory would purchase from, produce in, sell to, employ and improve the lives of local residents. Each factory would be designed to operate locally, keeping benefits within the community. The factories will rely on thousands of Grameen Bank microborrowers who buy cows and sell milk to each local plant. Grameen microvendors, mostly women on rickshaws, will sell yogurt door-to-door, making deliveries in a twenty-five to thirty kilometer radius from each factory to, among others, Grameen Bank savers and borrowers.

With respect to environmental sustainability, each factory will recycle materials, thereby generating a sufficient amount of biogas to supply energy to fifty local households. The yogurt will be sold in biodegradable cups made from cornstarch. Solar panels will provide electricity for each factory, which will also use rainwater collection vats.

To minimize expenses, each local factory will not have a marketing budget. Rather, the yogurt will be promoted by word-of-mouth recommendations.

For Danone, the joint venture offers the prospect of expanding into new markets with nutrition-enhancing products. Danone gets a good press, a sustainable business, and new markets hooked on the firm's products. After it gets its investment back, for Danone all of these positives are free.

Positive public relations, Gates's recognition factor, serves a bonus for Danone, but it is much more than that. Over the next decade, one billion people worldwide will become first-time consumers of goods. The so-called "bottom of the pyramid"[12] represents a huge commercial opportunity for both profit-maximizing and social businesses. It offers potentially breakthrough innovations in product offerings, distribution techniques, and pricing strategies, rather than simply offering overengineered and overpriced western brands in these markets. As the Grameen-Danone joint venture illustrates, reaching the bottom of the pyramid requires a re-engineering of an entire business, including the supply chain as well as the production and marketing processes.

Expanding the Social Business Concept

Unable to get started or grow because of a lack of access to capital, at present, social businesses generally find it hard to obtain funding from investors. Other obstacles stand in the way of the formation and growth of social enterprises. Their rules may differ from for-profit businesses, for example, with each shareholder having only one vote, regardless of the number of shares he or she owns. The market for shares is illiquid; disclosure is limited. The inability to sell their shares and the lack of regular reports deter many potential investors from considering social enterprises. A need also exists for high-quality, investment-ready social business opportunities.

To meet the capital needs of social businesses, Yunus envisions a new type of intermediary, a social equity capital market.[13] As a social stock market, it would offer opportunities for individual and institutional investors, including foundations, thereby providing a new source of funds for social enterprises.

Today, traditional equity capital markets focus on profit maximization centered on increasing shareholder monetary value, often built around a short-term perspective and a speculative approach. These capital markets do not look to social outcomes. The narrow outlook of traditional equity capital markets often undermines broader objectives, both social and environmental.

To fill the capital gap, a need exists to develop new mechanisms to help social businesses raise capital. The social capital field requires an infrastructure, the equivalent of stock market, together with the various other financial intermediaries, such as, investment bankers, research houses, and an independent rating system to evaluate social enterprise investment opportunities.

A social equity capital market would enable social enterprises to tap new capital sources. No longer would these firms need to rely on philanthropic support, or persuade the public sector to take on their endeavors to have a widescale impact.

A social equity capital market would link social enterprises with like-minded investors who not only want to champion a favorite cause or two but also want to see more regular reporting of operations as well as enhanced liquidity in the trading of social purpose shares. The price of shares would be measured in terms of the social benefit produced (or likely to be generated) by an entity, not its profits, past or future. In short, a social stock market would not only function to improve disclosure and governance standards by these entities but also shareholder liquidity. It also offers the possibility of expanding the range of social investment vehicles and raising the public awareness of social enterprises.

Numerous questions abound when considering the creation and operation of a social equity stock market.[14] These include both the entry criteria for a company to be listed on a social stock market and the exit criteria for a firm to lose its listing status. How would the exchange handle companies with a social mission but those that also achieve, perhaps not initially but over a period of years, significant profits and want to make distributions to investors? Other questions include: how to define a social business; how to (and who would) accredit a social business; what form would a social audit take? Also, would the new market mechanism take the form of: corporations bearing a designated label; a registered subgroup of firms on an existing stock exchange; or the creation of a separate exchange (or Internet mechanism) that lists businesses dedicated to the "social good" but offering little or no financial returns for investors? What would it cost to list a social business on an exchange and comply with the requisite reporting and disclosure obligations?

Models currently exist for a social equity capital market. In 2003, Bovespa, Brazil's stock exchange, created a Social Stock Exchange to match various nonprofit organizations looking for financial resources with donors seeking to provide them with funds.[15] Charities listed on this exchange establish how much money they need to raise for specific projects, initially educational in nature, but now broadened to include environmental endeavors. Investors buy social shares online in one or more projects they are interested in helping. Instead of paying investors a dividend, the organizations return a "social profit," by having a positive impact on sustainable development poverty alleviation in Brazil.

As the intermediary, the Bovespa coordinates the Social Stock Exchange's operations, without any charges, thereby providing credibility, transparency, security, and accountability for all donations. The social investors track the progress of a chosen project via the Bovespa's website. As projects succeed in obtaining the desired funds, they leave the exchange, making room, in turn, for new fundraising ventures.

Even if a social equity capital market were to be established in the United States, a need would exist for patient investors willing to support businesses that produce profits and social benefits.[16] It is unclear how many investors, although seeking social objectives, are willing to invest in enterprises that reinvest all of their profits (or offer only a modest distribution as a dividend). Although affluent individual investors clearly exist who want blended returns, let alone broader social objectives coupled with only the repayment of their investment, how many of them are there and how much capital are they willing to invest to achieve various social goals? Such individuals likely comprise only a minute segment of the investing public at present. Some of the world's wealthy and those not necessarily super-rich may be interested in funding social enterprises, that is, sustainable, nonloss, nondividend businesses. However, most of the aging baby boomers likely want the highest possible returns, coupled with a degree of safety, to fund their retirement. Thus, social business will probably depend on a "doing good"-kindness factor in attracting investments.

Beyond individual and institutional investors generally, foundations may provide a source of funds for social enterprises operating in a variety of fields, including microcredit, healthcare, renewable energy, and nutrition for the poor. Viewing investments as more akin to donations, foundations may see the benefits generated by recycling funds allocated to social firms.

A social stock market poses other problems for investors and social business executives. For investors, social benefits are difficult to quantify and may take decades to attain. Also, it is unclear whether the ventures will be sustainable over the years.

Even if executives find investors, who are aligned with a firm's social objectives and share a long-term perspective, not short-term speculation for financial gain, how will managers protect their control position in their firms? As exemplified by The Body Shop, acquired by L'Oreal, and Ben & Jerry's swallowed up by Unilever, social enterprises may sell out to larger entities and lose their social missions once they are acquired.

Social innovation is taking place through the structural transformations analyzed in this book, particularly the hybridization of philanthropy. The pace of change may accelerate in the future. Wealth holders see that often the traditional models of philanthropy are not working. Considerable time and money has been devoted to trying to solve social problems; however, the results thus far are meager, in the United States and globally.

People, particularly the wealthy, are looking beyond the public sector and private businesses to achieve social and environmental goals. It is unclear whether for-profit businesses or even social enterprises can successfully solve societal problems. Also, it is uncertain whether social businesses will be able to tap investors and generate earned income or will continue to be reliant on philanthropic or public sector support.

What is clear, however, is that the traditional categories of business and philanthropy may no longer serve to meet the challenge of social problems. In the twenty-first century, the tools and resources used to solve societal problems will be far more varied and mixed than previously. We likely will see some interesting partnerships and new ways of thinking. The divide between profit and social good will narrow. If successful in using their money in innovative ways, the government and for-profit businesses could scale up the catalytic efforts of the new philanthropists.

Notes

1. In a landmark article, Michael E. Porter and Mark R. Kramer, "Philanthropy's New Agenda," *Harvard Business Review* 77:6 (November-December 1999): 121-130, 121-122, 127-129, described many of the flaws in America's private foundations.
2. Dalia Fahmy, "Business-suited philanthropists," *Financial Times* (London), May 22, 2007, 1; Vartan Gregorian, "The Charity Chain," *Forbes* 179:10 (May 7, 2007): 240-241, at 240; Stephanie Strom, "Charities Try to Keep Up With the Gateses," *New York Times*, January 14, 2007, Section 1, 14; *The Economist*, "Rockefeller Revolution," 381:8508 (December 16, 2006): 68. See also, Porter and Kramer, "Philanthropy's New Agenda," 123-127, 130.
3. Bill Gates, "A New Approach to Capitalism in the 21st Century," January 24, 2008 <*http://www.microsoft.com/Presspass/exec/billg/speeches/2008/01-24WEFDavos.mspx?*> (January 27, 2008). See also Robert A. Guth, "Bill Gates Issues Call for Kinder Capitalism," *Wall Street Journal*, January 24, 2008, A1.

4. Andrew Carnegie, *The Gospel Of Wealth And Other Timely Essays*, ed. Edward C. Kirkland (Cambridge, MA: Belknap Press of Harvard University Press, 1962), 28 and Andrew Carnegie, "The Gospel of Wealth," in *The Responsibilities of Wealth*, ed. Dwight F. Burlinggame (Bloomington, IN: Indiana University Press, 1992), 11.
5. Muhammah Yunus with Karl Weber, *Creating a World Without Poverty: Social Business and the Future of Capitalism* (New York: PublicAffairs, 2007), 37-39, 40, summarizes the various sources of talent and funding for social businesses.
6. or capitalism as a "half-developed" structure, see Yunus, *Creating a World*, 18-19.
7. Yunus, Creating A World, 21-30; Muhammad Yunus, "Nobel Lecture," December 10, 2006 <*nobelpeaceprize.org/eng_lect_2006b.html*> (December 11, 2006) (reprinted in Yunus, *Creating a World*, 237-248); Muhammad Yunus, "National Press Club Luncheon Address," November 20, 2006 (Lexis Nexus); Muhammad Yunus, "Social Business Entrepreneurs Are the Solution," March 2006. See also David Greïsing, "'Social Business' the Next Big Idea," *Chicago Tribune*, January 27, 2008, Perspective Section, 4; Stephanie Strom, "Make Money, Save the World," *New York Times*, May 6, 2007, Section 3, 1. Critical assessments of social enterprises are provided by Ben Casselman, "Why 'Social Enterprise' Rarely Works," *Wall Street Journal*, June 1, 2007, W3; *Financial Times* (London) Report—Corporate Citizenship and Philanthropy, " Dividing lines are becoming blurred," July 5, 2007, 13; Seedco Policy Center, "The Limits of Social Enterprise: A Field & Case Analysis," June 2007.
8. Yunus analyzes the negatives of relying on charity and the built-in ceiling to the reach and effectiveness of nonprofit organizations in *Creating a World*, 9-11. See also Emily Parker, "The Weekend Interview with Muhammad Yunus," *Wall Street Journal*, March 1-2, 2008, A9.
9. In *Creating a World*, ix-xvii, 129-137, Yunus discusses the origins of the Grameen-Danone joint venture. See also Sheridan Prasso, "Saving the World One Cup of Yogurt At a Time," *Fortune* 155:31 (February 9, 2007): 96-102; Vikas Bajaj, "Out to Maximize Social Gains, Not Profit," *New York Times*, December 9, 2006, B4; Nutraceutical International, "Danone Bangladeshi Project Doing Well" (March 1, 2007): 26.
10. Andres Oppenheimer, "Nobel Winner's 'Social Businesses'," *Miami Herald*, March 25, 2007, A16.
11. Yunus discusses the implementation of the joint venture in *Creating a World*, 137-147, 149-161.
12. C.K. Prahalad, *The Fortune Act At The Bottom Of The Pyramid: Eradicating Poverty Through Profits* (Upper Saddle River, NJ: Wharton School Publishing, 2005); Allen L. Hammond and C.K. Prahalad, "Selling to the Poor," *Foreign Policy* 142 (May 1, 2004): 30-37; C.K. Prahalad, "Why Selling to the Poor Makes for Good Business," *Fortune* 150:10 (November 15, 2004): 70-72. But see Aneel Karnani, "Fortune at the Bottom of the Pyramid: A Mirage," Ross School of Business Working Paper Series, Working Paper No. 1035, September 2006.
13. Yunus, *Creating a World*, 181-184.
14. See generally, Charities Aid Foundation and New Economics, "Developing a Social Equity Capital Market 2006."
15. A case study, "BOVESPA and the Social Stock Market: Mobilizing the Financial Market for Development," October 2004, by Danielle Zandee <*http://unglobalcompact.org/newsandevents/news_archives/2000*> (May 22, 2007), details the evolution, role, and functioning of the Social Stock Exchange in Brazil. In

2006, the Johannesburg Stock Exchange adopted a program similar to Bovespa's Social Stock Market. See also R. Magliano Filho, "Stock Exchanges: Promoting Social Inclusion and Investment," *Compact Quarterly* 1:3 (July 2005) <*http:www.enewsbuilder.net/globalcompact/e_articles00425504*> (September 25, 2007) and Nicole Wallace, "International Gathering Seeks to Give 'Social Investing' Mass Appeal," *Chronicle of Philanthropy* 18:13 (April 20, 2006): 26-27, 30, at 30.

16. Yunus, *Creating a World*, 167-169, surveys who will invest in social businesses.

Index

Accelerate Brain Cancer Cure, Inc.
  Case Foundation, 99
  concept, 99
Accountability, 3, 31-32, 47, 126
Acumen Fund Inc.
  Acumen Fund Fellows Program, 113
  Google Foundation, 113
  in general, 73-74
  investment approach, 74
  Sandberg, Sheryl, 113
  Skoll Foundation, 74
Allen, Paul G., 15
AltaVista, 108
America Online, Inc., 85
America's Giving Challenge
  Case Foundation, 100
  concept, 100
AOL Time Warner, 85-86, 88-89, 110

Ben & Jerry's, 134
Benetech (Beneficent Technology, Inc.)
  Bookshare, 75
  Bookshare.org, 75
  business model, 75
  human rights software, 75
  Omidyar Network, 75
  Skoll Foundation, 75
Bill & Melinda Gates Foundation Asset Trust, 21
Bill & Melinda Gates Foundation
  Alliance for a Green Revolution in Africa, 31
  areas of interest, 15, 22-25, 30
  assessment, 29-32
  assets, 9, 17, 19-20
  benchmarks for success, 31-32
  Buffett, Warren E., 15, 19-20, 21
  economic opportunity, 25-27
  education, United States, 5, 22
  funding, 17, 19-20
  GAVI, 24

  Global Alliance for Vaccines and Immunizations, 24
  Global Development Program
    agricultural production, 25
    Financial Services for the Poor, 25
    sanitation, 25
    water, 25
  Global Health Program
    advocacy, 23
    approach, 22
    global health strategies, 22
    global health technologies, 22
    HIV/AIDS, 23
    infectious diseases, 22
    malaria, 23, 25
    policy endeavors, 22
    reproductive health, 22
    research, 22, 30
    tuberculosis, 22, 30
    vaccines, 23-24
  Grand Challenges Explorations, 24
  Grand Challenges in Global Health Initiative, 23-24
  grants, 22-25, 27-29
  healthcare, 22-25
  in general, 5, 15, 17-18
  Institute for OneWorld Health, 74
  International Finance Facility for Immunization, 24
  investments, 20
  microcredit institutions
    Pro Mujer, 27-28
    Unitus, 28-29
  Opportunity International USA, 34
  Pacific Northwest, 15
  partnerships, 31
  performance management, 31-32
  poverty alleviation, 25, 27-29
  Pro Mujer, 27-28
  ProCredit Holding, 34
  public health, 5, 15, 22-25

public schools, 15, 22
purposes, 19, 21
risk-taking, 30-31
scientific challenges, 22-23, 31
strategic vision, 30
targeted grants, 30
technology, 23
Third World, 15, 22-29
time limit, 21
traditional foundation model, 5, 15, 20-21, 29-30, 35
trustees, 21
tuberculosis, 22, 30
United States Program, 22
Unitus, Inc., 28-29
values, 17-18
Binswanger, Ben, 97
BlueOrchard Finance S.A.
  BlueOrchard Microfinance Securities 1, LLC, 55
  concept, 55
  Developing World Markets Microfinance LLC, 55
  loan funds, 55
  Omidyar Network, 55
  Overseas Private Investment Corp., 55-56
  securitization, 55
Body Shop, The, 134
Bottom of the pyramid, 131
Bovespa, 132
BrainTrust Accelerator Fund, 99
Brilliant, Larry
  background, 114
  Cometa Networks, 114
  Google.org, 114, 118
  inSTEDD, 117-118
  microfinance, 119
  Salon.com, 114
  SoftNet Systems Inc., 114
  TED Prize, 117
  The Well, 114
Brin, Sergey
  background, 108-109
  corporate philanthropy, 6, 107, 110, 111-112
  corporate philosophy, 110
  Doerr, John, 52
  Google Inc., 6, 109-112, 120
  Google.org, 6, 107, 111, 114-115, 118, 119-120

hybrid philanthropy, 3-4
in general, 6
net worth, 108
Omidyar, Pierre, 52
Page, Larry, 4, 6, 52
Stanford University, 108
Yunus, Muhammad, 52
See also *Google.org*
Buffett, Warren E.
  Berkshire Hathaway, Inc., 15
  in general, 5, 15
  Gates Foundation
    contribution to, 19-20
    trustee of, 21
Bunch, Jim, 56

Carnegie, Andrew
  career, second, 3
  Carnegie Corporation of New York, 11
  Carnegie Endowment for International Peace, 11
  Carnegie Foundation for the Advancement of Teaching, 11
  Homestead mill, strike at, 10
  in general, 3, 5, 10-11, 128
  libraries, funding of, 11
  megafoundation, 11
  Social Darwinian, 10
  "The Gospel of Wealth," 10, 11, 128
Carnegie Corporation of New York, 10
Case, Daniel H. (Dan) III, 87, 90, 99
Case, Jean, 100
See also Stephen Case Foundation
Case, Stephen M.
  America Online, Inc., 85
  AOL, 85, 87-88
  AOL Time Warner, 85-86, 88-89
  Apple Computer Inc., 87
  Apple Link, 87
  background, 86-89
  business empire, fall of, 88
  business empire, rise of, 87-88
  business strategy, 89-90
  Case III, Daniel H. (Dan), 87, 90, 99
  Case, Jean, 100
  CompuServe, 87
  Davis, Donn M., 89, 93
  entrepreneurship, 86, 89-90
  for-profit business, mission-driven, 6, 89-96
  GEnie, 87

innovative philanthropy, 100-101
hybrid philanthropy, 3-4, 6, 86, 97-99
Klain, Ronald, 90-91
Maui Land & Pineapple Company, Inc.
  in general, 98-99
    Kapalua Resort, 98
    Kapalua Ritz-Carlton Resort, 99
    Sustainable Living Institute of Maui, 99
PC-Link, 87
Pepsi Co's Pizza Hut, 86
Proctor & Gamble, 86
Prodigy, 87
Quantum Computer Services Inc., 87
Radio Shack, 87
social purpose business, 4
Tandy Corp., 87
Time Warner, 88
Von Meister, William, 87
See also Stephen Case Foundation; Revolution LLC; Revolution Health Group; Revolution Living LLC; Revolution Resorts
Center for Budget and Policy Studies, 119
Cisco Systems Foundation, 73
Climate Savers Computing Initiative, 116

Davenport, Tim, 93
Davis, Donn M., 89, 93
Develop Renewable Energy Cheaper Than Coal
  concept, 118
  investments, 118
Donors Choose
  concept, 49
  Omidyar Network, 49
DoubleClick, Inc., 110

eBay
  acquisitions, 45
  concept, 43, 45, 46-47
  corporate philanthropy, 70
  Craigslist, 45
  Giving Works, 98
  in general, 5, 45-47, 69-70
  MissionFish, 98
  Omidyar, Pierre, 45-47, 68, 70, 81
  PayPal, 45
  Skoll, Jeffrey, 69-70, 79, 81
  Skype, 45

social mission, 69-70
Whitman, Margaret (Meg), 45, 69
eBay Foundation, 70
eSolar Inc., 117, 118
Energy Efficiency Resource Standard, 117

Facebook, 100
Fahey, Richard, 67-68
Filmanthropy, 6, 76-81
Fiorina, Carly, 92
Forbes, 1, 16, 43, 67, 86, 108
Ford Foundation
  assets, 9
  program-related investments, 34
Fox Interactive Media, 110
Fuel the Growth of Small and Medium-Sized Enterprises
  concept, 119
Google.org, 119
GAVI, 24
Gates Learning Foundation, 17
Gates Library Foundation, 17
Gates, Melinda French, 17, 20, 21, 22
  See also Bill & Melinda Gates Foundation
Gates, William H. (Bill) Jr.
  Allen, Paul, 15
  antitrust suit, 18
  background, 16
  BASIC, 16
  Buffett, Warren E., 15, 19-20, 21
  creative capitalism, 6, 127-128
  DOS, 16
  Bill & Melinda Gates Foundation, 5
  Gates Learning Foundation, 17
  Gates Library Foundation, 17
  Harvard University, 16
  Harvard University commencement address, 22
  IBM, 16
  in general, 5, 15-16
  inequity, 21-22
  Microsoft, 15, 16
  MS-DOS, 16
  MS-DOS program, 16
  net worth, 16
  Patterson, Tim, 16
  science, 23
  Seattle Computer Products, 16
  technology, 23

140   Tech Billionaires

See also Bill & Melinda Gates Foundation and Bill & Melinda Gates Asset Trust
Gates, William H. Sr., 17, 21
Global Alliance for Vaccines and Immunizations
  concept, 24
  Gates Foundation, 24
Global Health and Security Initiative, 119
Global Warming Solutions Act of 2006, 117
Google Checkout, 110
Google Earth, 109
Google Foundation
  Acumen Fund, 113
  concept, 110, 111
  funding of, 111
  grants, 113-114
  One Laptop Per Child, 113
  Seva Foundation, 113
  TechnoServe, Inc., 113
Google Grants Program
  Doctors Without Borders, 114
  Grameen Foundation USA, 114
  in general, 113-114
  Make-a-Wish Foundation, 114
Google Inc.
  acquisitions, 109-110
  AdSense, 110
  AdWords, 110
  An Owner's Manual for Google's Shareholders, 110
  corporate Mission, 110
  corporate Philanthropy, 107, 110
  corporate Philosophy, 107, 110
  in general, 4, 6, 107, 110
  initial public offering, 109
  renewable energy sources, 117
  Sandberg, Sheryl, 107, 113, 115
  Schmidt, Eric, 109
Google.org
  areas of interest, 112, 114-119
  Brilliant, Larry, 114, 117-118, 119
  Center for Budget and Policy Studies, 119
  climate change, alleviating, 115, 116
  Develop Renewable Energy Cheaper Than Coal, 118
  concept, 107, 110-111
  eSolar, 117, 118
  established, 110-111
  Fuel the Growth of Small and Medium-Sized Enterprises, 119
  grants, 116-119
  in general, 6, 107, 111-112
  Information and Empowerment to Improve Public Services, 119
  investments, 116, 118
  lobbing, 112, 116-117
  Makani Power, 117, 118
  Pacific Gas & Electric, 116
  Page, Larry, 107, 110-113, 114-115, 118-120
  plug-in autos, commercialization of, 116
  Pratham, 119
  Predict and Prevent, 119
  rationale for, 111-112
  renewable energy sources, 117, 118
  RE<C, 117
  RechargeIT, 115-116
  TechnoServe, 119
"The Gospel of Wealth," 10, 128
Grameen Bank
  Grameen Danone Foods Ltd., 129
  Yunus, Muhammad, 25, 43
Grameen Danone Foods Ltd., 129-131
Grand Challenge Explorations, 23-24
Grand Challenges in Global Health Initiative, 23-24

Hybrid philanthropy, 3-4, 6, 43, 48, 86, 97-99, 134

inSTEDD
  concept, 117-118
  Google.org, 117
Institute for OneWorld Health
  concept, 74
  Gates Foundation, 74
  Skoll Foundation, 74
Internal Revenue Service
  Form 999-PF, 35
  Tax Exempt & Government Entities Division, 19
International Consumer Electronics Show, 87
International Development Law Organization
  concept, 58
  Omidyar Network, 58

International Finance Facility for Immunization, 24
Investment Company with Variable Capital, Danone Communities Fund, 130

J. Paul Getty Trust, 9
Johns Hopkins Medical School, 12

K-12 public education, 5, 15, 22, 49
Keyhole, Inc., 109
KickStart International, Inc.
  Case Foundation, 100
  concept, 75
  Skoll Foundation, 75
Kleiner Perkins Caufield & Byers, 52, 109

Leverage, 3
Lilly Endowment Inc., 9
Lycos, 108

Makani Power Inc., 117, 118
Megafoundations
  Carnegie Corporation, 10, 11, 126
  Gates Foundation, 9, 15, 19, 126
  impact, 12, 126
  Rockefeller Foundation, 10, 126
  transformation, 12, 126
Metrics, 3
Microcredit organizations
  assessment, 26-27, 61-62
  benefits, 26, 51-52
  concept, 25-26
  Grameen Bank, 25
  services offered, 27
  Yunus, Muhammad, 25
Microfinance, 26-27, 51-62, 119
Microfinance Information eXchange, Inc. (MIX)
  concept, 57
  Omidyar Network, 57
Microfinance institutions
  assessment, 26-27
  concept, 26, 54
  Omidyar, Pierre, 27-28, 51-62
Microfinance lending, 25-26, 51-54, 61-62
Microfinance organizations
  assessment, 26-27, 61-62
  benefits, 26, 51-52, 127
  concept, 26, 53-54
  services offered, 27
Microsoft, 15, 16, 44, 85, 110
MissionFish
  concept, 98
  Case Foundation, 98
Mission-related investment, 20
Murray, Mike, 28
MySpace, 110

Negropointe, Nicholas, 113

Omidyar Foundation
  creation, 47
  Omidyar, Pierre, dissatisfaction with, 47
Omidyar Network
  Ashoka, 49
  BlueOrchard Finance S.A., 55-56
  Brin, Sergey, 52
  Center for Effective Philanthropy, The, 49-50
  Clinton Global Initiative Conference, 51
  concept, 48
  Developing World Markets Microfinance, LLC, 55
  digg, 51
  DonorsChoose, Inc., 49
  GlobalGiving Foundation, The, 50
  grants, 49-50, 56-58
  hybrid philanthropy, 5
  Microfinance Information eXchange, Inc. (MIX), 57
  in general, 5, 48-49
  InnoCentive, Inc., 51
  International Development Law Organization, 58
  investments, 50-51, 54-56
  KaBOOM!, 50
  Linden Lab, 51
  microfinance intermediaries, 54-56, 61
  microfinance organizations
    assessment, 61-62
    concept of, 51-54
    grants to, 56-58
    investments in, 54-56
  Emission, 48-49
  Modest Needs Foundation, 50
  Omidyar Network Fund, Inc., 48
  Omidyar Network, LLC, 48
  Omidyar Services, LLC, 48

Page, Larry, 52
Prosper Marketplace, Inc., 50-51
Rare, 50
Second Life, 51
Socialtext, Inc., 51
Third World economic development, 51-54
Unitus Equity Fund, L.P., 56
Unitus, Inc., 56-57
YouthNoise, 50
Omidyar, Pamela, 47
Omidyar, Pierre M.
  Apple Computer Inc., 4
  auction concept, 4
  AuctionWeb, 4
  background, 4
  Bacow, Lawrence, 4
  Brin, Sergey, 4
  Claris, 4
  Doerr, John, 4
  eBay, 1, 3, 4
  empowerment, 4
  entrepreneurship, 4
  eShop, 4
  Feedback Forum, 4
  Gates, Bill, 3
  General Magic, 4
  Google.org, 7
  hybrid philanthropy, 1, 4
  in general, 1
  Ink Development Corp., 4
  microfinance, 4
    concept of, 4, 8
  microfinance organizations, concept of, 51-54
  Microsoft Corp., 44
  Omidyar Foundation, 47
  Omidyar Network, 48-51, 54-58
  Omidyar-Tufts University Microfinance Fund, 58-61
  opportunity, creation of, 48
  Page, Larry, 52
  Silicon Valley, 44
  Skoll, Jeffrey, 68, 69, 81
  Smith, Adam, 46
  trust, 46-47
  Tufts University, 58-59
  Whitman, Margaret (Meg), 45
  Yunus, Muhammud, 43-44, 52-54
  Zeitinger, C.P., 60-61
  See also Omidyar Foundation, Omidyar Network, Omidyar-Tufts University Microfinance Fund
Omidyar-Tufts University Microcredit Fund
  Bacow, Lawrence, 58
  board of trustees, 58
  concept, 58-59
  Evans, Tryfan, 59
  in general, 5
  investments, 59-61
  Omidyar, Pierre, 58-60
  ProCredit Holding AG, 60
  purposes, 59
One Laptop Per Child Foundation, 113
Opportunity International USA
  concept, 34
  Gates Foundation, 34
Oxford University, Said Business School, 76

Pacific Gas & Electric Co., 116
Page, Carl Jr., 108
Page, Larry
  background, 108-109
  Brin, Sergey, 4, 6, 52
  corporate philanthropy, 107, 110, 111-112
  corporate philosophy, 110
  Doerr, John, 52
  Google Inc., 6, 109-112, 120
  Google.org, 6, 107, 111-112, 114-115, 117, 118-119, 120
  hybrid philanthropy, 3-4
  in general, 6
  net worth, 108
  Omidyar, Pierre, 52
  Stanford University, 108
  Yunus, Muhammad, 52
  See also *Google.org*
Participant Productions
  American Civil Liberties Union, 78
  "An Inconvenient Truth," 78
  "Charlie Wilson's War," 78
  Clooney, George, 80
  concept, 77, 80-81
  Cuban, Mark, 79
  "Fast Food Nation," 78
  Federal Violence Against Women Act, 78
  "Good Night, and Good Luck," 78
  Gore, (Al) Gore, Jr., 78

Moore, Michael, 78
"Murderball," 78
"North Country," 78
Paramount, 79
participant.net, 79
Sierra Club, 78
social issues campaign, 79
"Syriana," 78
  script, evaluation of, 77-78
"The Kite Runner," 78
Warner Bros. Entertainment, 79
Partnerships, new, 4, 31, 134
Philanthrocapitalists, 1
Philanthropists, new
  rivalry, 4
  value added by, 6, 125-126
Philanthropulism, 100
Philanthropy
  brand-enhancing, 6, 131
  recognition factor, 127
PlayPumps
  Case Foundation, 97
  concept, 97-98
  funding, 97-98
Powell, Colin L., 92
Pratham, 119
Predict and Prevent, 119
Private foundations
  statistics on, 9-10
  tax aspects, 18-19, 32-35
  Washington State law, 19
Pro Mujer
  concept, 28
  Gates Foundation, 28
ProCredit Holding AG
  concept, 60
  Gates Foundation, program-related
    investment, 34
  Omidyar-Tufts University Microfinance
    Fund, 60
  Zeitinger, C.P., 60-61
Program-related investments, 34
Prosper Marketplace, Inc.
  concept, 50-51
  Omidyar Network, 52
Public health
  Gates, Bill, 12, 15, 22-25, 30
  Google.org, 7
  in general, 5
  Rockefeller, John D. Sr., 12

Raines, Franklin D., 92
RE<C
  concept, 117
  Google.org, 117
RechargeIT
  concept, 115
  Google.org, 115-116
RediClinic LLC
  advantages, 92
  Case, Stephen, 92
  concept, 92
Recognition factor, 127
Reicher, Dan, 116
Revolution Health Group LLC
  1-800 Schedule, 91
  CarePages, 93
  concept, 90-91
  Extend Health Inc. (formerly Extend
    Benefits LLC), 91
  HealthTalk, 91
  InterFit Health, 92
  MyDNA Media, 91
  RediClinic LLC, 92
  RevolutionHealth.com, 91
  Revolution Health Network, 93
  Simo Software, Inc., 91
  SparkPeople, 91
  TLContact, 91
  WebMD.com, 91
  Wondir Inc., 91
Revolution Living LLC
  Flexcar, 95
  in general, 94
  Lime-Healthy Living with a Twist, 94
  Miraval Resort and Spa
    Center for Life in Balance, 94
    concept, 94
    O'Donnell, Bill, 94
    Ruff, George, 94
    Weil, Andrew, M.D., 94
  Wisdom Media Group, Inc., 94
  Zipcar, 95
Revolution LLC, 6, 89
Revolution Money
  concept, 95-96
  GratisCard Inc., 95
  Revolution Card, 96
  Revolution Money Exchange, 96
Revolution Resorts
  Revolution Places, 93-94
  Exclusive Resorts, 94

Miraval, 94
Exclusive Resorts LLC
  concept, 93
  Handler, Brad, 93
  Handler, Brent, 93
RevolutionHealth.com, 91
Robert Wood Johnson Foundation, 9
Rockefeller Foundation
  Acumen Fund, 73
  Alliance for a Green Revolution in Africa, 31
  assets, 10
  creation, 2, 12
  Gates Foundation, 31
Rockefeller, John D., Sr.
  career, second, 3
  General Education Board, 12
  in general, 3, 5, 11-12
  megafoundation, 12
  Rockefeller Foundation, 10, 12
  Rockefeller Institute for Medical Research, 12
  Standard Oil, 11-12
  University of Chicago, 12

Sandberg, Sheryl, 107, 113, 115
Scalability, 3, 52, 53, 62
Securitization, 55
Self-empowerment, 43, 46, 48, 51, 53
Sequoia Capital, 109
Seva Foundation
  Brilliant, Larry, 114
  concept, 114
  Google Foundation, 113
Shah, Rajiv J., 27
Skoll Awards for Social Entrepreneurship, 73
Skoll Centre for Social Entrepreneurship
  concept, 76
  Skoll Fellows, 76
  Skoll Scholars, 76
  Skoll World Forum on Social Entrepreneurship, 76
Skoll Community Fund, 71
Skoll Foundation
  Acumen Fund Inc., 73-74
  Benetech, 75
  focus, 71
  grants, analytical factors, 72-73
  in general, 5-6
  Institute for OneWorld Health, 74

  KickStart International, Inc., 75
  long-term funding, 5-6, 71
  Skoll Awards for Social Entrepreneurship, 76
  social entrepreneurs, 71-76
Skoll, Jeffrey
  1984, 68
  AuctionWeb, 69
  background, 68-69
  Brave New World, 68
  eBay, 5, 69-70
  father, 2
  filmanthropy, 76-81
  "Gandhi," 67
  gifts, time of, 1-2
  in general, 5-6
  inequality, 68, 70
  Knight-Ridder Information, Inc., 69
  Lewis, Richard Barton, 77
  Michener, James, 68
  Micros on the Move, Ltd., 69
  motion pictures, 68
  net worth, 67
  Omidyar, Pierre, 68, 69, 81
  optimism, 67
  Ovation Entertainment, 77
  Participant Productions, 76-81
  Rand, Ayn, 68
  Silicon Valley Community Foundation, 71
  Skoll Community Fund, 71
  social entrepreneurs, 71-76
  Stanford University, 69
  Zachary, George, 77
  See also Participant Productions and Skoll Foundation
Skoll World Forum on Entrepreneurship, 76
Social businesses
  Acumen Fund, 73-74
  concept, 128-129
  funding sources, 128-129, 131, 139
  in general, 6-7
  obstacles, 131
Social Edge, 76
Social entrepreneurs
  concept, 5-6, 72
  funding, 71-75
  Skoll Awards for Social Entrepreneurship, 73
  Skoll Foundation, 71-76

Index

Skoll, Jeffrey, 71
Skoll World Forum on Entrepreneurship, 76
Social enterprises
  Acumen Fund, 73-74
  concept, 128-129
  funding sources, 128-129, 131, 139
  in general, 6-7
  obstacles, 131
Social purpose business, 4, 128-131
Social Stock Exchange, 132
Social stock market
  benefits, 131-132
  concept, 132
  in general, 7
  questions, 132-133
Solomon, Doug, 56
Stephen Case Foundation, The
  Accelerate Brain Cancer Cure, Inc., 99
  America's Giving Challenge, 100
  assets, 96
  BrainTrust Accelerator Fund, 99
  Case, Jean, 100
  grants, 97-100
  Habitat for Humanity, 99
  Hawaii Community Foundation, 99
  hybrid approach, 97-99
  innovative approaches, 100-101
  MissionFish
    concept, 98
    Giving Works, 98
    Points of Light and Hands on Network (Points of Light Foundation), 98
  PlayPumps, 97-98
  PONO (Promoting Outstanding Nonprofit Organizations) Leadership Program, 99
  Roundabout Outdoor, 97-98
  strategic themes, 96
  University of Hawaii Business Plan Competition, 99
Supporting organization, 71
Sustainability, 52, 53, 62, 72, 96

Tax aspects, private foundations
  distributions, 33
  donors, 18-19
  excess business holdings, 33
  excise tax, 19, 32-34
  exempt organization returns, 35

jeopardy investments, 33-34
oversight, 19
program-related investments, 34
self-dealing, 32
taxable expenditures, 35
Tech billionaires
  gifts, timing of, 1-2
  impatient, 4
  involvement, 2-3
  philanthropy, impact on, 1-4
  strategy, 3
  tactics, 3-4
  See also Brin, Sergey; Case, Stephen; Gates, Bill; Omidyar, Pierre; Page, Larry; Skoll, Jeffrey
TechnoServe, Inc.
  concept, 113
  Google Foundation, 113
  Google.org, 119
TED (Technology, Entertainment, Design) Prize, 117
Third World
  corruption, 128
  disease, 5, 15, 22-25
  economic development, 5, 25-27, 30, 51-62, 119
  prosperity, path to, 127-128
Time Warner, 85, 88
Traditional foundation model, 5, 10-12, 15, 20-21, 29-30, 35
Transparency, 31-32

Unitus Equity Fund, L.P.
  concept, 56
  Omidyar Network, 29, 56
Unitus, Inc.
  concept, 28-29, 56-57
  Gates Foundation, 28
  microfinance organizations, assessment, 57
  Omidyar Network, 56-57

Von Meister, William
  Case, Stephen, 87
  Control Video Corp., 87
  Digital Music, 87
  Quantum Computer Service Inc., 87
  Q-Link, 87
  The Source, 87

WebMD.com, 91

Whitman, Margaret (Meg), 45, 69
William and Flora Hewlett Foundation, 9
William H. Gates Foundation, 17
W.K. Kellogg Foundation, 10

YouTube, 110
Yunus, Muhammad
  background, 52
  Chittagong University, 52
  Grameen Bank, 25, 43, 129
  Grameen Danone Foods Ltd., 129-131
  Groupe Danone SA, 129-131
  microcredit concept, 25-26, 52-53
  microcredit organizations, 27, 52-53
  Nobel Peace Prize, 25, 43
  Omidyar, Pierre, 27, 52-54
  social enterprises, 6-7, 128-131

Zeitinger, C.P., 60-61